HILARIOUS HOLIDAY HUMOR

FOR KIDS

Santa's Giggle Factory:

A Collection of Holiday Humor

Alex Reynolds

TABLE OF CONTENTS

INTRODUCTION

"Hilarious Holiday Humor for Kids: Santa's Giggle Factory – A Collection of Holiday Humor" welcomes you to its fantastic universe. In the enchanting corridors of Santa's Giggle Factory, laughter is the key ingredient, and merriment is the order of the day. This delightful e-book is designed to be a festive companion for kids during the holiday season, ushering them into a realm where joy knows no bounds and laughter echoes through the snowy landscapes.

The holiday season is a time of magic, wonder, and traditions, and what better way to celebrate than with a hearty dose of laughter? A hilarious treasure trove, "Santa's Giggle Factory," gives kids a front-row ticket to the hilarious antics at the North Pole. From jolly jokes about Santa's adventures to mischievous tales of Santa's elves causing delightful mayhem, this collection is crafted to tickle the funny bones of young readers.

Within these pages, kids will discover the amusing side of holiday decorations, the rib-tickling antics of snowmen, and the loud happenings during the gift-wrapping extravaganza. The e-book transforms familiar holiday elements into sources of laughter, making each chapter a portal into a festive wonderland where the ordinary becomes extraordinary through the lens of humor.

Set out on an adventure across the snow-covered terrain of the North Pole, where reindeer tell jokes, snowmen engage in spirited conversations, and Santa's elves orchestrate merry mischief. As kids immerse themselves in the tales of Santa's Giggle Factory, they will find themselves giggling, chuckling, and perhaps even laughing out loud. This compilation celebrates the joy that humor provides to the holidays, not merely a list of jokes.

Prepare for an entertaining sleigh ride where each page leads to more joy, laughter, and holiday spirit. More than merely a compilation of jokes, "Hilarious Holiday Humor for Kids: Santa's Giggle Factory" extends an invitation to partake in the heartwarming moments that give the holidays their unique flavor. Get ready for a festive adventure that will leave kids of all ages with smiles as bright as Rudolph's nose. Welcome to Santa's Giggle Factory, where the magic of laughter transforms the holiday season into a truly unforgettable experience.

CHAPTER 1

Jolly Jokes for Little Elves

Light-hearted Santa Jokes

The holiday season brings a unique brand of joy and merriment, and at the heart of this festive spirit is Santa Claus himself. As the embodiment of generosity and goodwill, Santa has become an iconic figure synonymous with Christmas celebrations. However, amidst the serious business of gift-giving and spreading cheer, a delightful realm of humor exists – the world of light-hearted Santa jokes.

These jokes are a great way to inject cheer into the season and are commonly told around the fireplace or at a festive feast. Picture a group of friends and family gathered near a Christmas tree's sparkling lights, their laughter echoing through the air as they exchange these whimsical tales. The essence of these jokes lies in their ability to evoke smiles and laughter, momentarily transporting individuals from the stresses of everyday life to a world filled with warmth and amusement.

One of the classic motifs in light-hearted Santa jokes revolves around the jolly older man's penchant for overindulging in milk and cookies. "Why did Santa go to the doctor?" goes one joke. "Because he had low 'elf' esteem!" The play on words brings a chuckle and taps into the playful imagination of envisioning Santa discussing his self-worth with a medical professional. This combination of innocent wordplay and the familiarity of Santa's character makes these jokes so endearing.

The humor extends beyond the North Pole, weaving into the logistics of Santa's Christmas Eve journey. "What do you call Santa when he takes a break? Santa Pause!" This clever play on words pokes fun at the notion of Santa taking a breather and introduces a linguistic twist that tickles the funny bone. In these light-hearted jabs at the logistics of Santa's magical night, we find a shared understanding of the notion that encapsulates the holiday season.

Furthermore, these jokes often draw on the juxtaposition of Santa's magical abilities with more mundane elements of daily life. "Why was Santa's helper depressed? Because he had low 'elf' esteem!" This joke not only continues the 'elf' humor theme but also humanizes Santa's helpers, imbuing them with relatable emotions. Through these jokes, Santa and his team of elves become not just mythical beings but characters with feelings and quirks that resonate with our own experiences.

Santa's legendary status as a gift-giver provides ample material for playful banter. "What do you get if you cross Santa with a detective? Santa Clues!" In this instance, the joke cleverly combines Santa's iconic image with the world of mystery and investigation. This ability to seamlessly merge disparate elements into a cohesive, humorous narrative defines the charm of light-hearted Santa jokes.

Moreover, the cultural and global appeal of Santa Claus opens the door to a diverse array of jokes that transcend borders. "Why did Santa's helper see the doctor? Because he had low 'elf' esteem!" With a slight variation, this joke illustrates the universality of humor associated with Santa, making it accessible and enjoyable for people from different cultures and backgrounds. It is a testament to the enduring nature of Santa's character as a unifying figure during the festive season.

As we delve into the realm of light-hearted Santa jokes, it becomes evident that they serve as more than mere entertainment. They act as a bridge between generations, creating shared moments of laughter and contributing to the tapestry of holiday memories. The simple act of exchanging these jokes fosters a sense of camaraderie, bringing people together through the universal language of laughter.

Furthermore, the lighthearted nature of these jokes offers a respite from the sometimes overwhelming nature of the holiday season. "What do you call Santa when he takes a break to sing? Santa Pause!" The pun in this joke not only references a pause in Santa's duties but also introduces the joyous element of singing. It is a gentle reminder that amidst the hustle and bustle, it's essential to take a moment to pause, enjoy the festivities, and burst into song.

The enduring popularity of light-hearted Santa jokes also resides in their capacity to cross age boundaries. Whether young or old, these jokes appeal to the childlike wonder the holiday season instills. "What do you call Santa when he loses his pants? Saint Knickerless!" The innocence and playfulness of this joke evoke a sense of nostalgia, harking back to a time when the magic of Santa captivated our imaginations.

In addition to bringing joy to individuals, these jokes play a role in reinforcing the positive image of Santa Claus. "What do you call Santa on the beach? Sandy Claus!" This playful pun places Santa in an unexpected setting and highlights the adaptability and good-natured spirit we associate with the legendary gift-giver. It is a reminder that Santa's magic isn't confined to the snowy landscapes but extends to wherever the spirit of giving is embraced.

The tradition of sharing light-hearted Santa jokes also mirrors the evolution of humor in society. While the essence of these jokes remains timeless, their delivery may evolve to reflect contemporary themes and trends. "What do you call Santa when he takes a selfie? Santa Paws!" This modern twist introduces the concept of selfies, bringing Santa into the digital age. It is a testament to the versatility of these jokes, demonstrating their ability to stay relevant while maintaining the core elements that make them so endearing.

In conclusion, light-hearted Santa jokes play a crucial role in enhancing the festive atmosphere during the holiday season. Through clever wordplay, playful scenarios, and a touch of magic, these jokes bring people together, fostering a sense of joy and unity Let us keep this in mind when we assemble around the Christmas tree and not forget the power of laughter and the simple pleasure derived from a well-timed Santa joke. In the spirit of the season, may these lighthearted jests continue to bring smiles to faces, creating lasting memories filled with the magic of Christmas.

Reindeer Riddles

In the enchanting of holiday traditions, "Reindeer Riddles" emerge as whimsical threads, weaving an air of mystery and laughter into the festive atmosphere. The charming reindeer, Santa Claus's regal companions, not only carry gifts on their merry voyage but also bring joy and laughter. These riddles, cleverly designed to tickle the intellect and ignite smiles, transform the reindeer from stoic sleigh-pullers into the charismatic jesters of the North Pole.

Imagine Rudolph, with his luminous nose aglow, posing a riddle to his fellow reindeer: "What do you call a reindeer with no eyes?" The answer, "No eye-deer!" echoes with a double entendre that transcends the realm of puns and lands squarely in the land of hilarity. In Reindeer Riddles, wordplay becomes a vehicle for joy, turning these majestic creatures into endearing characters with a penchant for jest.

Reindeer riddles are beautiful because of their ingenious designs and their capacity to unite the fantastical and the ordinary. As children and adults alike engage with these riddles, they find themselves transported to the North Pole, where reindeer, despite their extraordinary abilities, share a sense of camaraderie and a delightful sense of humor. The riddles become a vessel, carrying us into a realm where the whimsical and the everyday coalesce in laughter.

The intelligent simplicity of these riddles, whose solutions frequently involve wordplay or creative linguistic twists, is something one cannot but admire. In one puzzle, the query is, "What do you call a reindeer that tells jokes?" The response, "A comedian," makes the reindeer seem like a lively character with a sense of humor in addition to making you laugh. It's as though the reindeer find comfort and delight in the common language of laughter on their difficult voyage around the globe.

These riddles also offer a delightful exploration of the personalities of individual reindeer, giving them distinct identities beyond their roles in pulling Santa's sleigh. They develop into clever friends with different qualities and a sense of humor beyond being gift-givers. Through the lens of Reindeer Riddles, the reindeer become characters in a comedy routine, contributing to the festive ambiance with their quick wit and clever repartees.

These puzzles also capitalize on the ageless allure of anthropomorphism by giving the reindeer human characteristics that humanize and humanize them. By seeing the reindeer joking around and using witty wordplay, we can go beyond the realm of the fantastic and connect through the universal language of comedy. The riddles bridge the mystical and the every day, inviting us to see the reindeer as mythical creatures and companions with a delightful sense of humor.

Reindeer Riddles are a charming game that serves as a reminder of the importance of comedy during the holiday season. Laughter, often hailed as the universal language, becomes a unifying force that transcends age, culture, and background. These riddles become conduits for shared joy, creating moments of connection as families and friends gather to solve the playful enigmas. In their newfound role as jesters, the reindeer bring people together through the simple act of laughter.

In the educational realm, Reindeer Riddles assume an additional layer of value. These puzzles serve as instruments for children's cognitive growth, encouraging critical thinking and linguistic inventiveness in addition to being entertaining. Deciphering the wordplay, understanding the nuances of language, and arriving at the punchline contribute to linguistic and cognitive skills. Under the pretense of entertainment, the riddles serve as instructional aides, drawing young minds into a lighthearted language investigation.

With their clever constructions and witty punchlines, Reindeer Riddles also provide an avenue for cultivating a positive and lighthearted mindset. During a season frequently filled with stress and obligations, these puzzles serve as a helpful reminder to tackle difficulties with humor. In their playful roles, the reindeer encourages us to find joy in the unexpected, appreciate the art of clever wordplay, and navigate life's complexities with a smile.

The cultural resonance of Reindeer Riddles is evident in their enduring popularity across generations. These puzzles span time and geography, bridging the gap between past and present traditions, and are as ageless as the customs they go along with. They become a link in the chain of festive businesses, passed down from generation to generation, creating a sense of continuity and shared merriment.

With its capacity to amplify shared experiences, social media has played a role in revitalizing the charm of Reindeer Riddles. Platforms like Instagram and Pinterest showcase creative adaptations of these riddles, inviting a global audience to participate in the joyous exploration of humor. The hashtag #ReindeerRiddles becomes a digital gallery where individuals from diverse corners of the world come together to share laughter and celebrate the wit of these endearing creatures.

In conclusion, Reindeer Riddles are luminous beacons of laughter in the festive night sky. They urge us to participate in a lighthearted word dance with the reindeer, where comedy and ingenuity are the main attractions. Beyond their role as jesters, these riddles contribute to the cultural tapestry of the holiday season, creating moments of connection, cognitive engagement, and shared joy. As we gather around the fireplace, with the glow of holiday lights illuminating our faces, let the Reindeer Riddles spark laughter and merriment, turning the season into a delightful journey of enigmatic cheer.

Frosty the Snowman Shenanigans

In the whimsical world of winter wonderlands, "Frosty the Snowman Shenanigans" add a playful and mischievous touch to the season's magic. Frosty, that lovable and animated snowman with a corncob pipe and a button nose, becomes not just a static figure in the snowy landscape but a dynamic character engaged in a series of delightful antics. Through these antics, Frosty transforms from a representation of winter happiness to a lively and mischievous friend in the realms of frost-kissed adventures. The storyline of these antics is cheerful.

Imagine Frosty, wearing his enchanted hat, tiptoeing across the scenes, dusted with snow as the moon shines silver. In "Frosty the

Snowman Shenanigans World," the ordinary transforms into the extraordinary, and the snowman takes on his own life. Their antics' storyline embodies Frosty's lighthearted nature, ranging from the joyful to the downright ridiculous.

It is easy to see Frosty playing a game of snowball hide-and-seek, his snowy form perfectly blending into the icy surroundings. Children and adults participate in a story where the snowman is more than simply a static sculpture—he is a living character full of mischief and joy—as they imagine Frosty's fun adventures. The snowball fights and friendly pranks celebrate winter's delight, where the laughter of Frosty echoes through the crisp air.

Beyond the traditional imagery of Frosty as a stationary snowman, these shenanigans breathe life into his character, making him a mischievous companion in the snow-covered playgrounds of the imagination. In one scenario, Frosty might be caught dancing with the winter wind, his snowy form twirling and swaying in a whimsical ballet. These antics add layers to Frosty's persona and infuse the winter landscape with a sense of animation and magic.

The mischievous nature of Frosty's escapades extends to interactions with other winter residents. Imagine Frosty engaging in a spirited conversation with a snow owl perched on a frosty branch or playfully teasing a snow rabbit as it hops through the snowy meadows. In these situations, Frosty becomes a well-balanced member of the winter ecology, providing a festive atmosphere and fostering relationships with the charming animals of the snow-covered forests.

As we delve into the realm of "Frosty the Snowman Shenanigans," it becomes evident that Frosty is not just a static figure but a symbol of the dynamic spirit of winter. His playful misadventures serve as a reminder that winter is a time for vibrant celebrations rather than a time for lethargy. Through the lens of Frosty's antics, the snowy landscape transforms into a canvas for joy and laughter, with the snowman at the center of the recreation.

These antics also speak to the enduring popularity of Frosty, a figure that both kids and adults like. The naughty side of Frosty adds a layer of relatability, making him more than a seasonal decoration but a friend who joins in the laughter and playfulness of the holiday season. The image of Frosty engaging in snowball fights or whimsical conversations becomes a shared narrative that transcends generational boundaries.

In the cultural lexicon, Frosty has become synonymous with the joy of winter and the holiday season's festivities. The song "Frosty the Snowman," with its catchy tune and cheerful lyrics, has ingrained Frosty's image as a merry and animated snow companion. The shenanigans attributed to Frosty, whether in song or the imagination, become extensions of this cultural narrative, contributing to the collective celebration of winter's whimsy.

The mischievous nature of Frosty's escapades has found new life in the digital age, with creative reinterpretations and adaptations proliferating on social media platforms. Instagram and TikTok become virtual stages for Frosty's antics, where users share illustrations, animations, and short videos depicting the snowman's playful adventures. The hashtag #FrostyShenanigans becomes a digital gallery of creativity, connecting people worldwide to celebrate Frosty's animated spirit.

Furthermore, Frosty's mischievous escapades have become a source of inspiration for winter festivals and celebrations. In communities worldwide, events centered around Frosty the Snowman feature live performances, parades, and interactive displays that capture the animated spirit of the beloved character. These festivities turn the playful shenanigans of Frosty into communal celebrations, where families and friends gather to share the joy of winter's merriment.

Frosty's cheeky side is also a metaphor for winter's spontaneity and unpredictable nature. Like the ever-changing patterns of snowflakes and the unpredictability of a snowstorm, Frosty's shenanigans remind us that winter is a season of surprises and delights. His playful escapades become a representation of the magic inherent in the frosty landscapes, where each snowfall brings with it the potential for joyous mischief.

In conclusion, "Frosty the Snowman Shenanigans" transforms the iconic snowman into a dynamic and mischievous figure, weaving a narrative of winter whimsy. Frosty's button nose and corncob pipe become a lively participant in the seasonal celebrations, engaging in snowball fights, playful dances, and whimsical conversations with the creatures of the winter woods. These antics give Frosty more nuance and give the winter scenery a lively, cheery vibe. As we revel in Frosty's mischievous escapades, we celebrate winter's magic, where laughter echoes through the snowy realms, and the snowman becomes a symbol of the season's animated delight.

CHAPTER 2

Elf Antics and
Mischievous Moments

Tales of Santa's Mischievous Elves

In the enchanting realm of holiday folklore, "Tales of Santa's Mischievous Elves" emerge as delightful narratives that add a whimsical layer to the magic of Christmas. These tales take us to the busy workshops at the North Pole, where Santa's hardworking little assistants, dressed in festive green and red, make gifts with diligence and indulge in fun activities that add cheer and cheer to the holiday season. These mischievous elves, with their pointy ears and impish grins, become more than just Santa's assistants; they are the spirited architects of laughter in the festive tapestry of Christmas.

The stories usually begin with the elves painstakingly making toys, each with exacting attention to detail. However, it is not long before their mischievous nature takes center stage, turning the workshop into a hub of playful escapades. Picture an elf sneaking into the toy paint room and turning all the paint colors into a rainbow swirl, creating a kaleidoscopic array of hues that elicit laughter from the elves and Santa himself. These fun anecdotes transform into short

Christmastime stories that bring a lighthearted element to the hardworking ambiance of the North Pole.

One recurring theme in these tales is the elves' penchant for playful pranks on one another, creating a pleasant atmosphere that resonates with the camaraderie of the holiday season. From hiding tools to swapping hats, the elves engage in lighthearted schemes that transform the workshop into a place where laughter is as abundant as the snow outside. Far from causing chaos, these pranks contribute to the festive ambiance, turning the workshop into a haven of joy.

A recurring theme in the stories is the elves' infatuation with Santa's enchanted Naughty and Nice List. In their mischievous endeavors, the elves often playfully rearrange the names, causing momentary confusion and laughter among themselves. These episodes highlight the elves' curiosity and playfulness, reminding us that even those responsible for maintaining order in the holiday hierarchy can't resist the allure of a good-natured jest.

The mischievous nature of Santa's elves extends beyond the workshop into their interactions with the world beyond the North Pole. Some stories have the elves going on covert missions to bring holiday cheer to unknowing homes. Their playful antics include rearranging ornaments on Christmas trees, leaving whimsical notes for children, and even attempting to create a snowstorm of candy canes. These exploits cheer up the receivers and highlight the elves' goal of bringing wonder and excitement to the festive season.

These stories about mischievous elves are fascinating because they perfectly capture the spirit of the holidays. The naughty escapades, far from undermining the magic of Christmas, enhance it by infusing the season with lightheartedness and joy. In the grand tapestry of holiday traditions, the mischievous elves become catalysts for laughter, reminding us that amidst the hustle and bustle of preparations, the true magic of Christmas lies in moments of shared merriment.

Moreover, these tales serve as a reminder that the holiday season is not just about gift-giving and decorations; it is also a time for playful celebration and a touch of irreverence. The cheeky elves are the epitome of holiday cheer, inspiring us to enjoy the fun aspects of the season. Their pranks and playful antics become metaphors for the unexpected delights that the season brings, fostering an atmosphere of joy and surprise.

In popular culture, the naughty elves have become iconic figures, featuring prominently in holiday-themed movies, books, and decorations. From classic films to animated specials, the playful nature of Santa's elves has been immortalized on screen, becoming a beloved part of the cultural lexicon. The naughty elves entertain and serve as cultural ambassadors of the holiday spirit, spreading joy and laughter to audiences of all ages.

In recent years, the mischievous elves have found a new platform for their playful escapades—social media. Social media platforms like Pinterest and Instagram present imaginative and fun take on naughty elves in different environments, encouraging people to write their own Christmas comedy stories. The hashtag #MischievousElves becomes a digital gallery where users worldwide share and celebrate the antics of these festive troublemakers, creating a virtual community united by a love for holiday merriment.

One must recognize the educational value embedded in these tales of mischievous elves. The elves develop into personalities that provide important lessons about the importance of companionship, laughing, and accepting the unexpected, in addition to their function as entertainers. The playful pranks and adventures become allegories for life's surprises, encouraging children and adults alike to approach challenges with humor and playfulness.

Through their stories, the mischievous elves further emphasize that the holidays are a time for bonding and shared experiences. Whether it's the elves collaborating on an evil plan or spreading joy to households worldwide, their stories emphasize the importance of coming together to celebrate the magic of Christmas. The playful misadventures serve as a reminder that the holidays are a communal celebration of joy, laughter, and the spirit of giving rather than merely a set of occasions.

To summarize, "Tales of Santa's Mischievous Elves" provides a festive touch to the holiday season, not only fantastical accounts of mischievous playmates. These tales transport us to the heart of the North Pole, where industrious elves, with a twinkle in their eyes, engage in playful antics that spark laughter and spread holiday cheer. Whether in traditional literature, film adaptations, or contemporary social media posts, the naughty elves have become essential to

Christmas culture, personifying the joyous festivity that characterizes the season's magic. As we delve into these tales, we embrace the mischievous spirit of Santa's helpers and rediscover the timeless joy that comes from shared laughter and the magic of the holiday season.

Elf on the Shelf Hilarities

In the realm of festive enchantment, "Elf on the Shelf Hilarities" weaves a whimsical tapestry of laughter and playfulness, adding a touch of mischievous magic to the holiday season. The Elf on the Shelf, that diminutive scout Santa's messenger assigned to monitor kids' behavior, becomes not just a watchful overseer but a spirited companion engaged in comical escapades. These tales of Elf on the Shelf hilarities have transcended the realm of holiday tradition, becoming a cherished narrative that infuses homes with laughter and delight during the festive season.

The idea is straightforward but charming: every night, the Elf on the Shelf goes around the house, adopting new positions and situations, and when kids wake up, they find out about the elf's most recent mischievous activities. This naughty tradition has captured the hearts of families worldwide, transforming the elf into more than just a festive spy but a source of endless amusement.

Imagine waking up to find the Elf on the Shelf perched on a miniature zipline, gliding from the curtain rod to the Christmas tree, or perhaps engaged in an impromptu marshmallow snowball fight with other toys. These creative and humorous scenarios, designed by parents and caretakers, turn the elf into a dynamic and playful character, creating a sense of anticipation and excitement for children each morning.

One of the joys of Elf on the Shelf hilarities is the element of surprise. Children look forward to playing hide-and-seek with the naughty elf as he goes about his daily adventures, looking for him in all the different corners of the house. Every new finding elicits yells of delight and laughter, transforming the everyday grind into a joyous journey full of unexpected turns.

The mischievous nature of the Elf on the Shelf is not just for the delight of children; it also taps into the creative spirit of parents and caretakers. Crafting imaginative scenarios for the elf requires a blend of ingenuity and playfulness, transforming the home into a canvas for holiday whimsy. From creating scenes of the elf baking tiny cookies in the dollhouse kitchen to orchestrating a miniature movie night with popcorn and doll-sized DVDs, the possibilities for Elf on the Shelf hilarities are as boundless as the imagination.

Families can connect creatively and enjoy each other's company while participating in these silly pranks over the Christmas season. Parents and children collaborate on the daily escapades, brainstorming ideas and bringing the elf to life in a way that reflects the unique personality of their household. The joint endeavor becomes a type of festive teamwork that promotes camaraderie and celebration.

Elf on the Shelf jokes capture the essence of seasonal customs that transcend decades, even beyond the heartfelt amusement they arouse.

With its mischievous charm, the elf becomes a shared character in the family's festive narrative, creating memories that endure over time. As children grow older, the tales of the elf's antics become cherished stories that evoke nostalgia and a sense of continuity in the ever-evolving landscape of holiday celebrations.

Social media platforms have significantly increased the cultural phenomenon of Elf on the Shelf hilarities. Instagram and Pinterest, in particular, serve as virtual galleries where families showcase their creative and humorous takes on the elf's daily adventures. The hashtag #ElfOnTheShelfIdeas becomes a digital community where individuals worldwide share and celebrate the imaginative and often hilarious scenarios they've crafted for their mischievous elves.

The cheeky personality of the Elf on the Shelf reflects the worldwide appeal of happiness and good humor throughout the holidays. In a world where obligations and deadlines abound, the Elf on the Shelf serves as a humorous reminder to savor the happiness of the here and now. The elf's antics pause the daily routine, encouraging families to share a collective laugh and appreciate the magic of the holiday season.

Furthermore, the Elf on the Shelf hilarities introduces an element of wonder and magic to the narrative of Santa's helpers. The elf may be responsible for watching kids' behavior, but its mischievous antics foster friendship and teamwork. The elf becomes more than a mere enforcer of Santa's Naughty and Nice List; it is a playful confidant, engaging in whimsical adventures that cultivate a feeling of unity and joy that is shared.

In conclusion, "Elf on the Shelf Hilarities" contributes a generous dose of merriment to the holiday season, turning a simple tradition into a source of laughter and creative expression. The Elf on the Shelf's malicious behavior transforms homes into stages for holiday whimsy, where each new day brings a fresh surprise and a shared moment of joy. As families across the globe welcome this pint-sized sprite into their homes, they partake in a tradition that celebrates the magic of Christmas and emphasizes the timeless importance of laughter, creativity, and togetherness during the festive season.

Snowball Fights at the North Pole

In the wintry expanse of the North Pole, where stretches of snow-covered terrain are visible for the entire distance, a spirited tradition unfolds each year that transcends the ordinary frosty scenes—Snowball Fights. While the North Pole may be more commonly associated with Santa's workshop and his bustling team of reindeer, the addition of lively snowball skirmishes introduces a playful and communal element to the snowy terrain. These frosty showdowns, far from being mere pastimes, become an integral part of the festive tapestry, blending the season's magic with the joyous camaraderie born from the simple pleasure of a snowball fight.

Imagine Santa's assistants, the pleasant and hardworking elves, coming out of the workshop wearing their festive winter attire. Equipped with snowballs and wearing hats as colorful as the Aurora Borealis, they turn the peaceful surroundings into a battlefield of joy and laughter. The snowball fights at the North Pole, with their origins lost in the frosty annals of time, have become a cherished tradition that unites the community in a shared celebration of winter's merriment.

The snowball fights, often initiated by the playful elves, unfold in the sprawling landscapes surrounding Santa's workshop. The snow-laden fields and evergreen forests witness the gleeful chaos as elves duck behind snowbanks, giggling and plotting their strategic maneuvers. The sound of laughter, snowballs swishing through the air, and the muffled thuds of well-aimed projectiles hitting their snowy targets reverberate in the fresh Arctic air.

What makes the snowball fights at the North Pole genuinely enchanting is the participatory nature of the event. Santa himself, with his red cheeks and loud chuckle, frequently gets involved in the icy debate, personifying the festive attitude of joy that characterizes the Christmas season. The reindeer, usually dignified in their roles as sleigh-pullers, eagerly prance through the snow, their antlers adorned with tinsel, as they observe the playful antics with a twinkle in their eyes.

The snowball fights become a communal spectacle, bringing together the North Pole residents in a shared winter festivity experience. Mrs. Claus, with her apron dusted in flour from the day's baking, steps outside to cheer on the playful combatants. The workshop's resident polar bears, often overlooked as guardians of the snowy expanse, amble through the fields, their fur coated in glistening frost, to observe the merriment.

Even though they are lighthearted, the snowball fights at the North Pole have more profound meaning. They serve as a communal release, a lighthearted interlude amid the busyness of holiday preparations. The snowball fights provide a break from the chaos of producing toys and wrapping presents, allowing the people of the North Pole to relax, spend time together, and enjoy the small pleasures of winter.

In addition, the snowball fights help the people of the North Pole feel united. In a society where cooperation and teamwork are essential to the success of holiday planning, lighthearted conflicts take on symbolic meaning for joint ventures. The laughter that rings through the frosty air echoes the bonds forged in the workshop, emphasizing the importance of camaraderie and mutual support in the festive season.

The fact that snowball fights can be modified further illustrates how flexible holiday customs can be. While the North Pole may lack the quintessential snow days that children in other parts of the world eagerly await, the introduction of snowball fights brings a touch of that universal winter joy to the Arctic landscape. The custom serves as a reminder that the season's magic has no geographical bounds and embraces everyone who wants to join in on the exuberant celebrations.

In the age of social media, the snowball fights at the North Pole have found a digital stage. The hashtag #NorthPoleSnowballFights becomes a global gallery where individuals worldwide join in the celebration, sharing their winter escapades and reveling in the joyous tradition.

The snowball fights at the North Pole, with their spontaneous and exuberant nature, also resonate with the universal appeal of winter play. Across cultures, engaging in a snowball fight is a cherished tradition that spans generations. It captures the excitement of friendly rivalry, the delight of being outside in the brisk winter air, and the making of enduring memories with loved ones.

The snowball fights reach their climax as the sun dips below the icy horizon at the North Pole, casting a soft glow on the snow-covered landscape. Laughter and cheers fill the air as the playful skirmishes draw to a close. The fighters, breathless and with red cheeks, assemble to greet each other with grins and heavy back pats; their friendship is a tribute to the season's enduring vitality.

The snowball battles near the North Pole give the Arctic scenery a whimsical, magical quality that turns the white expanse into a canvas of winter celebration. Beyond their surface-level merriment, these frosty skirmishes embody the communal spirit of the holiday season, bringing together the residents of the North Pole in a shared celebration of winter's joy. The laughter, the camaraderie, and the timeless appeal of a snowball fight create a tradition that transcends the boundaries of age and geography, reminding us all that, in the heart of winter, there is a universal language of merriment that connects us all.

CHAPTER 3

Reindeer Humor
in the Winter Wonderland

Reindeer Jokes and Puns

In the enchanting world of holiday humor, "Reindeer Jokes and Puns" add a whimsical touch to the festive season, bringing joy and laughter to young and old alike. The mention of reindeer conjures images of Santa's loyal sleigh-pullers, with their majestic antlers and endearing names like Rudolph, Dasher, and Prancer. However, beyond their role in yuletide lore, reindeer become the charming protagonists of a repertoire of jokes and puns that infuse the holiday season with merriment.

The humor surrounding reindeer frequently focuses on their unique traits, cute eccentricities, and, of course, their essential function in creating the enchanted atmosphere of Christmas. Imagine a herd of reindeer congregating near the North Pole in a little tavern, giggling over hot chocolate and exchanging tales of their icy exploits. In these lighthearted jests, reindeer become more than mythical creatures; they are animated characters with a sense of humor that captivates the imaginations of those who revel in the festive spirit.

One recurring theme in reindeer jokes is the playful exploration of their antlered personalities. Antlers, those majestic crown-like features, become the subject of whimsical musings. A classic joke might ask, "Why do reindeer wear hats in the winter?" The punchline? "Because it's the only way to keep their antlers dry!" These jokes humorously humanize reindeer, giving them a sense of fashion and fun.

The most famous of Santa's reindeer, Rudolph, with his luminous red nose, takes center stage in many of these jokes. His glowing appendage becomes a source of playful banter, as jests like, "What did Santa say to Rudolph before they took off on Christmas Eve?" The answer? "Rudolph, light the way!" These one-liners capitalize on the well-known images connected to Rudolph, transforming his distinctive quality into a fun and lighthearted source of entertainment.

Jokes about reindeer also highlight the unity among Santa's sleigh pullers. The reindeer are portrayed as a close-knit team in these jests, sharing a bond forged through snowy adventures and festive escapades. An example might go, "Why did the reindeer form a band?" The punchline? "Because they had the drumsticks!" These jokes not only celebrate the unity of the reindeer team but also infuse the holiday narrative with a musical twist.

Another aspect of reindeer humor that makes people laugh and smile is puns, known for their witty wordplay. Using homophones and double entendres adds a layer of delight to the jokes. A classic reindeer pun might be, "What do you call a reindeer with no eyes?"

The playful answer: "No-eye-deer!" These puns showcase the light-hearted creativity surrounding the festive season, turning language into a canvas for delight.

Not only are reindeer jokes popular when said aloud, but they also impact visual humor. Cartoons, illustrations, and memes featuring whimsical reindeer scenarios abound on social media platforms, contributing to the collective laughter that permeates the digital landscape during the holidays. The hashtag #ReindeerJokes becomes a virtual gallery where individuals worldwide share and celebrate these playful jests, creating a global community united by a love for holiday hilarity.

Reindeer jokes are also enduringly popular because they make a connection with people of all ages. Whether told around a crackling fireplace during a family gathering or shared among friends at a festive party, these jokes bridge generational gaps, fostering a sense of shared joy. Reindeer humor is a universal language that cuts over linguistic and cultural barriers because of its simplicity and innocence, allowing everyone to join in on the fun.

In literature and popular culture, reindeer jokes have become integral to the narrative of the holiday season. Children's books, animated specials, and holiday-themed movies often feature endearing reindeer characters engaging in playful banter and humorous escapades. The charm of these jokes contributes to the timeless appeal of holiday classics, creating a sense of nostalgia and warmth that resonates with audiences year after year.

The fact that reindeer jokes are still popular shows how vital comedy is in creating a joyful mood. Amid holiday preparations, shopping, and the hustle and bustle, these jokes offer a delightful respite, reminding us to embrace the lighter side of the season. Laughter turns into a festivity, and the lighthearted jokes about Santa's reindeer spread a contagious joy throughout the atmosphere.

In conclusion, "Reindeer Jokes and Puns" are a cherished facet of holiday humor, adding a touch of whimsy to the festive season. Whether centered on antler antics, Rudolph's glowing nose, or the camaraderie of Santa's sleigh-pullers, these playful jests create a lighthearted narrative that resonates with people of all ages. Beyond their role in verbal banter, reindeer jokes become a cultural phenomenon, finding expression in visual mediums and social media, uniting individuals worldwide in a shared celebration of holiday hilarity. We participate in a timeless custom that connects people and fosters a sense of joy and camaraderie that characterizes the magic of the holiday season as we laugh heartily at these charming jokes.

A Comedy of Illumination

In the grand tapestry of life, where each moment is a stroke of color on the canvas of existence, a narrative thread emerges that weaves through the human experience—a Comedy of Illumination. This illuminating comedy unfolds as individuals navigate the complexities of self-discovery, enlightenment, and the pursuit of wisdom, often finding humor in the unexpected moments of illumination that light the path to a deeper understanding of life.

The Comedy of Illumination is a journey that takes characters from the shadows of ignorance into the radiant light of self-awareness. It is a journey filled with laughter, not as a mockery of ignorance but as a celebration of the human spirit's capacity to unravel the mysteries of existence. This story unfolds in acts like a well-written comedy, with each realization and epiphany as a punchline that makes the audience laugh heartily.

The script of the Comedy of Illumination is written in the language of self-discovery, where individuals grapple with the questions at the core of human existence. The pursuit of knowledge becomes a comedic exploration, with characters stumbling through the corridors of libraries, engaging in philosophical dialogues, and embarking on quests for enlightenment that often lead to unexpected and humorous revelations. The laughter accompanying these moments is not a dismissal of the seriousness of life's questions but a recognition of the delightful absurdity of seeking understanding in a vast and intricate universe.

In the Comedy of Illumination, humor is a torch to lead people through the maze of self-discovery. The ability to laugh at one's misconceptions, find amusement in the human mind's quirks, and embrace the humbling realization that enlightenment is an ongoing process creates a lighthearted atmosphere in the pursuit of wisdom. Laughter becomes the companion that lightens the weight of existential pondering, inviting individuals to approach life's profound questions with curiosity and playfulness.

The illumination in this comedic narrative is not confined to intellectual enlightenment alone. It extends to the realm of emotional intelligence and self-awareness. In this comedy, characters navigate the complexities of relationships, emotions, and the heart's inner workings while facing circumstances that reflect the human condition. The moments of illumination are not limited to grand epiphanies but often manifest in the subtle realization of the beauty and absurdity of the emotional landscape.

The Comedy of Illumination, much like a stand-up routine, introduces moments of paradox and irony. In their quest for comprehension, characters could discover that the unremarkable features of everyday existence frequently cover up the solutions they need. The revelation that wisdom can emerge from the most unexpected places—a casual conversation, a fleeting moment of observation, or a seemingly trivial experience—adds a layer of delightful irony to the narrative. The audience, whether the characters themselves or the readers witnessing the comedy unfold, is treated to the joyous recognition that enlightenment need not always come in grandiose gestures but can emerge from the tapestry of ordinary moments.

In the Comedy of Illumination, the role of the teacher often takes on a whimsical quality. Wisdom is not always imparted through sage advice or profound lectures but may instead be delivered through the antics of life itself. The world turns into the ultimate comic, giving thought-provoking and amusing teachings through the lens of everyday situations. Characters are placed in scenarios where the universe acts as a cunning mentor, imparting knowledge through life's unexpected turns and turns.

As the narrative arc of the Comedy of Illumination progresses, characters undergo a transformation that transcends the limitations of the mind and touches the soul. The illumination becomes a holistic experience, blending intellectual insight, emotional intelligence, and a deepening connection to the broader tapestry of existence. The laughter that accompanies these moments of enlightenment is not merely cerebral but resonates in the depths of the human spirit, creating a harmonious symphony of joy, understanding, and a profound appreciation for the mysteries of life.

The Comedy of Illumination is not without its share of challenges and trials. The agony of recognizing one's limitations, the vulnerability of facing the unknown, and the sobering awareness that wisdom is a path that never ends are all possible emotions for characters to experience. However, in these moments of vulnerability, the comedy finds its most poignant notes, offering a powerful reminder that the ability to laugh at oneself is an essential ingredient in the recipe for true enlightenment.

In the grand finale of the Comedy of Illumination, characters emerge not as solemn sages with all the answers but as humble beings who have danced through the illuminating comedy of life. The laughter that echoes through the corridors of understanding becomes a testament to the resilience of the human spirit, the beauty of embracing the unknown, and the joyous celebration of the ongoing journey of self-discovery. In this grand comedy, where the spotlight of wisdom illuminates the stage of existence, the characters and the audience alike are invited to revel in the joy of illumination, embracing the laughter accompanying the perennial pursuit of understanding in the grand theater of life.

Behind the Scenes at the Reindeer Talent Show

A fantastic event that brings a whimsical touch to the holiday season occurs in the enchanted land of the North Pole, where celebrations and magic abound. It's called the Reindeer Talent Show. While Santa's reindeer are renowned for their sleigh-pulling prowess, the talent show offers a behind-the-scenes glimpse into their diverse and often surprising abilities. This captivating event, held in a frosty arena adorned with twinkling lights, showcases the myriad talents of Santa's faithful companions, transforming the North Pole into a stage for laughter, applause, and the joyous celebration of reindeer ingenuity.

As the curtains rise on the Reindeer Talent Show, the audience, comprised of elves, snowmen, and even the occasional polar bear, eagerly anticipates the unexpected feats and performances that will unfold. The reindeer, adorned with jingle bells and festive accessories, prance onto the stage with a spirited energy that sets the tone for the evening. Instead of being a formal competition, the talent event becomes a joyful celebration of the distinct abilities and character traits that make up each member of Santa's sleigh team.

The first act unveils the comedic talents of the reindeer, with jesters and jokesters among them taking center stage. Antler acrobatics and hoof-tapping routines elicit laughter from the audience, setting a lighthearted atmosphere that resonates throughout the show. The humor is not limited to physical antics; some reindeer showcase their wit through clever banter and festive jokes, turning the talent show into a comedy extravaganza that uplifts spirits and brings joy to the North Pole.

Musical interludes become another highlight of the Reindeer Talent Show, with some reindeer demonstrating their melodic prowess. From antler percussionists creating rhythmic beats to vocal performances that echo through the wintry air, the musical acts add a harmonious dimension to the festivities. The sound of jingling bells and the melodic notes of holiday tunes fill the arena, creating a symphony of festive cheer that captivates the audience.

The Reindeer Talent Show is not without surprises; magical displays of holiday enchantment often take the spotlight. Imagine a reindeer conjuring snowflakes with a mere flick of its tail or another creating a dazzling array of Northern Lights through a choreographed dance. These enchanting acts, infused with the season's spirit, elevate the talent show into a magical spectacle that showcases the extraordinary nature of Santa's reindeer.

The backstage area, a whirlwind of activity and enthusiasm, demonstrates the reindeer's sense of cooperation. Some help their colleagues change into new costumes so that every performance is accompanied by a sight worthy of the holiday. Beyond the stage, the reindeer's fellowship fosters a sense of unity and shared delight that characterizes the North Pole festive season.

In addition to comedic and musical acts, the Reindeer Talent Show also features physical prowess and agility displays. Daring feats of antler balancing and hoof dexterity leave the audience in awe, showcasing the athleticism and grace of Santa's sleigh-pullers. These shows, which are frequently expertly planned, highlight the reindeer's adaptability and capacity to enthrall an audience with abilities beyond dragging sleds.

The talent show also allows the reindeer to express their individuality. Some have latent abilities beyond what one may assume from their sleigh-pulling roles. A reindeer may reveal a knack for painting festive scenes with hooves, or another surprise the audience with a stand-up comedy routine that leaves everyone in stitches. These times of self-discovery and expression provide the talent show a more intimate feel while letting each reindeer show off their brilliance.

The Reindeer Talent Show transcends the boundaries of species, with participation from other North Pole residents. The resident polar bears might engage in a synchronized snow dance, and the misfit toys, often overlooked during the festive season, find a place in the spotlight with heartwarming and endearing acts. The inclusivity of the talent show reflects the spirit of togetherness and celebration that defines the holiday season at the North Pole.

Even in the enchanted land of the North Pole, social media contributes to the charm of the Reindeer Talent Show. Elves are armed with enchanted smartphones to capture and share snippets of the performances, creating a virtual gallery of holiday cheer on platforms like Instagram and Snowbook. The hashtag #ReindeerTalentShow becomes a digital community where inhabitants of the North Pole and festive enthusiasts worldwide celebrate the talent show's magic.

As the final act concludes and the arena erupts in applause, the Reindeer Talent Show leaves an indelible mark on the holiday season at the North Pole. The laughter, cheers, and shared moments of joy reverberate through the wintry landscape, creating memories long after the curtain falls. The talent show evolves from a spectacle into a beloved custom that captures the spirit of the holidays—laughter, friendship, and the joy of finding the remarkable in the everyday.

In conclusion, the Reindeer Talent Show at the North Pole transcends the expectations associated with Santa's sleigh-pullers, offering a behind-the-scenes look at the diverse and enchanting talents that define each reindeer. The comedic, musical, and magical acts unfold in a festive atmosphere, celebrating individuality and togetherness. As the North Pole revels in the laughter and applause echoing from the talent show, it becomes clear that, beyond their role as sleigh-pullers, Santa's reindeer are magical performers who add a touch of whimsy to the holiday season, making it truly extraordinary.

CHAPTER 4

Christmas Decorations Shenanigans

Tangled Tinsel Tales

In the realm of holiday decorations, few elements embody the festive spirit as vividly as the glistening strands of tinsel. But hidden behind Tangled Tinsel Tales' glittering charm is a hilarious story that plays out every year, making decorating houses a delightful journey. As households worldwide delve into boxes of decorations, the level of tangled tinsel becomes a universal narrative. This shared experience blends frustration with laughter and imparts a sense of camaraderie as families navigate the intricacies of holiday adornment.

The tale begins innocently enough, with the anticipation of transforming living spaces into winter wonderlands. Boxes brimming with ornaments, lights, and seemingly innocent strands of tinsel await their moment in the spotlight. As the first gleaming strands emerge, there's a collective sense of excitement—a festive tradition about to unfold. Little do households realize that within those seemingly innocuous coils lies the potential for hilarity, exasperation, and the creation of lasting holiday memories.

When one tries to drape tinsel precisely, one soon discovers that these fragile threads have an independent will. The more detailed the scheme, the more complex the resistance of the glitz. It's as if the shimmering lines conspire to engage in a playful dance, weaving into an elaborate tapestry of knots and twists that defy the best-laid decorating schemes.

The comedy of Tangled Tinsel Tales lies in the physical challenge of unraveling these mischievous strands and the shared exasperation that accompanies the process. What starts as a planned attempt to make the celebration more joyful becomes a family project—an unanticipated ritual of camaraderie filled with jokes, laughter, and the odd friendly taunting.

Amid the untangling mayhem, the spirit of the season shines through. Families discover the joy of working together, navigating the labyrinth of tinsel with patience and shared merriment. A web of shimmering threads entangles parents and kids, yet instead of creating anger, the room is filled with the pleasant sounds of laughter and good-natured conversation.

Every year, the mishaps involving tangling tinsel give rise to festive tales that are exchanged and enhanced. The memory of Uncle Bob attempting to free himself from an incredibly clingy strand or the epic battle between siblings and a particularly stubborn coil becomes a cherished part of the family lore. Rather than being a source of annoyance, Tangled Tinsel Tales become a story that connects generations through common holiday mistakes.

Social media, ever attuned to the pulse of the holiday season, becomes a virtual stage for Tangled Tinsel Tales. Families share the everyday experience of battling mischievous tinsel by documenting their adventures with amusing pictures and videos. The hashtag #TangledTinselTales trends across platforms, creating a global community united by the laughter and camaraderie that arise from the shared challenge of adorning homes with these ornate yet elusive strands.

The comedic nature of Tangled Tinsel Tales is still in popular culture. Television shows, movies, and holiday specials often incorporate the theme of unruly tinsel into their narratives, further cementing its status as a universal holiday trope. Characters grapple with tinsel-induced chaos, adding a touch of realism to their fantastical worlds and allowing audiences to relate to the ensuing hilarity.

Beyond its comedic elements, Tangled Tinsel Tales also encapsulates the essence of holiday imperfection. In a season often idealized for its picture-perfect moments, the misadventures with tinsel become a reminder that the beauty of the holidays lies not in flawlessness but in the shared joy of the imperfect and the genuine. The disorganized chaos becomes evidence of the actual vacation experience, in which the trip is just as important as the destination.

As the last strand of tinsel is finally draped, the room bathed in the shimmering glow of holiday lights, a sense of accomplishment transcends the temporary chaos. With all its comedic twists and turns, Tangled Tinsel Tales transforms into a story of resilience, unity, and the triumph of festive spirit over momentary disorder. The glittering threads, which are already adorning homes in an adorable but disorganized manner, serve as a visual reminder that sometimes the most memorable holiday experiences come from the most unexpected places.

In conclusion, Tangled Tinsel Tales narrates a universal holiday experience, turning what may initially seem like a decorating debacle into a source of laughter, bonding, and cherished memories. The tinsel mishaps become a crucial part of the Christmas story as families worldwide participate in the yearly practice of decorating their houses. Far from being a mere decorative challenge, Tangled Tinsel Tales transforms into a shared comedy, uniting households in the delightful chaos that defines the festive season. Ultimately, it's not just about untangling strands—it's about weaving a tapestry of joy, laughter, and the timeless camaraderie that makes the holiday season truly magical.

Ornament Overload: When Baubles Go Wild

In the enchanting world of holiday decorations, a phenomenon turns embellishing trees into a whimsical adventure—Ornament Overload: When Baubles Go Wild. As households embark on the annual tradition of adorning Christmas trees with an array of ornaments, the line between tasteful festivity and exuberant excess blurs gives rise to a comedic narrative that transforms living rooms into kaleidoscopic wonderlands. The story of Ornament Overload delves deeply into the delicate equilibrium between the raucous joy of ornamentation and the cheerful excess of hanging ornaments.

As the story progresses, boxes full of decorations with special sentimental or thematic significance are revealed. From delicately handcrafted treasures passed down through generations to whimsical creations inspired by the latest holiday trends, the array of baubles mirrors the diversity of memories and experiences woven into the season's fabric. However, the potential for Ornament Overload lurks beneath the festive surface, waiting to be unleashed as families dive into the decorative process.

The initial placement of ornaments is a meticulous affair, with each family member contributing to the choreography of colors, shapes, and memories that will adorn the tree. However, as the excitement builds and the allure of ornament variety takes hold, the tree becomes a canvas for a kaleidoscopic explosion of festive exuberance. What begins as a careful arrangement transforms into a riot of colors, themes, and sizes as the baubles seem to take on their own life.

Ornament Overload stimulates every sensation; it's not just a pretty sight. The jingling of bells, the rustling of tinsel, and the clinking of glass ornaments create a symphony of festive sounds that resonate through the air. The intoxicating aroma of pine intermingles with the scent of cinnamon and cloves, heightening the sensory experience of the holiday extravaganza. Families find themselves surrounded by decorations and an immersive holiday atmosphere that transcends the ordinary.

The comedic charm of Ornament Overload lies in the realization that, amidst the merriment, the tree has become a visual feast, challenging even the most seasoned holiday enthusiasts to locate a square inch of greenery beneath the festive finery. It's a beautiful disarray, evidence of the zeal with which each item was selected and the joy with which it was arranged. The formerly meticulously chosen tree now serves as a symbol of the overwhelming joy of the holidays.

The decorative enthusiasm spills to nearby surfaces as the tree reaches its Ornament Overload zenith. Mantels, windowsills, and even furniture become secondary canvases for overflowing baubles. Every available space in the living room becomes a joyous paradise, ready for any decoration. Rather than being a source of frustration, this exuberant overflow becomes a visual feast that envelops the entire space in the warmth of holiday cheer.

Social networking sites transform into online galleries where families gleefully display their works of Ornament Overload art. Photos of lavishly adorned trees, each more dazzling than the last, flood timelines and create a shared celebration of festive exuberance. As people worldwide join in, sharing and enjoying the joyous excess that characterizes the holiday season, the hashtag #OrnamentOverload becomes popular.

The comedic elements of Ornament Overload extend beyond visual spectacle to the practical challenges it presents. Watering the tree or retrieving a fallen ornament from the lower branches becomes a whimsical obstacle course. Families navigate a forest of baubles, gingerly treading through the decorative labyrinth that has taken over their living spaces. However, rather than being an obstacle, these difficulties become a part of the story of the joyous holidays.

Ornament Overload, however, is not just about the sheer number of decorations but also the stories they tell. Every ornament—painstakingly made or randomly selected—becomes a container for customs and recollections. Families recount tales associated with each bauble, from the handmade kindergarten crafts to the quirky travel souvenirs that found a place among the branches. In all its vitality, Ornament Overload becomes a celebration of the richness of family history and the continuity of holiday traditions.

As the holiday season progresses, Ornament Overload takes on a life of its own, transcending the individual households and becoming a collective phenomenon. Cities, towns, and public spaces embrace the festive excess, adorning streets and storefronts with abundant lights, baubles, and seasonal decor. The shared spirit of Ornament Overload becomes a unifying force, transforming communities into illuminated wonderlands that resonate with the season's joy.

In conclusion, Ornament Overload: When Baubles Go Wild is a delightful tale of holiday exuberance, where decorating transforms into a riotous celebration of festive abundance. The tree, adorned with many baubles, becomes a visual feast that embodies the enthusiasm and joy of the season. Beyond the visual extravaganza, Ornament Overload is a shared story that unites people worldwide in a communal holiday spirit celebration. As we revel in the riotous beauty of Ornament Overload, we embrace the timeless truth that, in the world of holiday decorations, more is indeed merrier, and the exuberance of festive abundance is a source of joy that transcends the ordinary.

The Great Christmas Tree Debate

In the heart of the holiday season, amidst the twinkle of lights and the aroma of freshly baked cookies, a spirited debate takes center stage—the Great Christmas Tree Debate. It is a lively discourse that unfolds in living rooms, community centers, and social media platforms as families and individuals grapple with the perennial question: to opt for a natural or artificial Christmas tree. This yearly dilemma explores traditions, sustainability, and the immersive experience that characterizes bringing a tree into one's house in addition to beauty.

For proponents of real Christmas trees, the allure lies in the authentic and time-honored tradition of selecting, chopping, or purchasing a living evergreen to serve as the festive centerpiece. The experience of visiting a tree farm, navigating rows of fragrant pines or spruces, and ultimately choosing the perfect specimen carries a sense of holiday ritual that transcends generations. For these enthusiasts, the Great Christmas Tree Debate is not merely about decoration but a journey steeped in tradition, where the process of acquiring the tree becomes as significant as its adorned presence.

The aroma of a real Christmas tree, permeating the home with its natural fragrance, adds another layer to the debate. When the smell of pine or fir fills the air, it becomes a sensory trigger that indicates the start of the holiday season. This fragrant experience creates a sensory link to treasured memories and customs, making it indispensable to the Christmas atmosphere for many. The debate, therefore, extends beyond visual aesthetics to encompass the immersive and multisensory nature of the Christmas tree experience.

However, the proponents of artificial trees are not without their convictions in the Great Christmas Tree Debate. Advocates for synthetic trees often cite practicality, cost-effectiveness, and environmental considerations as compelling reasons to opt for an artificial alternative. Reusing the same tree year after year attracts people looking for a more environmentally responsible and sustainable way to holiday traditions. The Great Christmas Tree Debate turns into a discussion about how decisions people make in the name of holiday cheer affect the environment.

Artificial trees, with their consistent shape and pre-attached lights, also offer convenience that resonates with modern lifestyles. Families assess the comfort of assembly, the absence of needle shedding, and the decreased fire hazard of artificial trees in this practical discussion. In a fast-paced world, where time is a precious commodity, the efficiency of an artificial tree becomes a persuasive factor in the decision-making process.

The Great Christmas Tree Debate extends its tendrils into the heart of family traditions. For some, selecting a real tree becomes a cherished annual event—a family outing filled with laughter shared memories, and the thrill of discovery. The search for the ideal tree turns into a tradition that strengthens family ties and fosters camaraderie. On the other side of the debate, families that assemble and decorate artificial trees together find joy in the collaborative effort, forging traditions that center around the home and the shared act of transforming it into a festive haven.

The visual aesthetics of natural versus artificial trees also play a significant role in the debate. Proponents of real trees often argue that nothing can replicate the authentic beauty of a living evergreen, with its unique shape, varying shades of green, and the natural irregularities that make each tree one of a kind. The debate becomes an exploration of individual tastes and preferences as families weigh the allure of a genuine, nature-inspired centerpiece against the uniformity of an artificial alternative.

One of the main points of dispute in the Great Christmas Tree Debate is the environmental impact. Real tree enthusiasts argue that their choice supports sustainable agriculture, as Christmas tree farms typically plant more trees than they harvest. Since genuine trees may be converted into mulch or compost after the holidays, the argument also applies to their biodegradability. On the contrary, advocates for artificial trees emphasize the longevity and reusability of their choice, contending that a well-maintained artificial tree can last for many years, reducing the need for repetitive production and disposal.

The debate also delves into the economic aspects of Christmas tree choices. Real trees, often grown locally, support small businesses and local economies. Buying a real tree contributes to the sustainability of tree farms and the farmers' means of subsistence. In contrast, the artificial tree industry, dominated mainly by manufacturing, relies on global production and distribution networks, raising questions about the carbon footprint associated with its mass production.

Social media platforms become battlegrounds for the Great Christmas Tree Debate, with individuals proudly showcasing their chosen trees and passionately defending their stance. Photos of real trees adorned with twinkling lights and homemade ornaments compete with images of perfectly shaped artificial trees boasting uniformity and pre-lit brilliance. Hashtags such as #RealTreeJoy and #ArtificialTreeMagic become rallying cries for advocates on either side, creating virtual communities that echo the sentiments of the more significant debate.

In conclusion, the Great Christmas Tree Debate is a nuanced and multifaceted discourse that transcends the simple choice between natural and artificial trees. It includes immersion in the festive season, tradition, beauty, and sustainability. Families and individuals, as they engage in this spirited conversation, reveal not only their preferences but also the values that shape their approach to the festive season. Ultimately, whether adorned with the scent of fresh pine or the convenience of pre-lit branches, the chosen Christmas tree reflects personal convictions, family traditions, and the enduring magic that defines the holiday spirit.

CHAPTER 5

Tree Trimming Laughs

Adventures in Christmas Tree Decorating

Embarking on the annual journey of Christmas tree decorating is not merely a festive tradition; it is an adventure that unfolds in living rooms across the world, transforming homes into holiday havens filled with twinkling lights, shimmering ornaments, and the timeless aroma of evergreen. Adventures in Christmas Tree Decorating are more than just decorating a tree; they're also a joyful investigation of artistic expression, cherished family customs, and the pure joy that results from everyone working together to bring magic to the holiday season.

The adventure begins with the tree selection, whether it be a towering evergreen sourced from a local tree farm or an artificial creation carefully stored from years past. Each tree promises to become a canvas for holiday magic, and the act of choosing sets the tone for the escapade that lies ahead. Families embark on this quest with a shared sense of anticipation, armed with boxes of ornaments, strings of lights, and a festive spirit that transforms the ordinary into the extraordinary.

As the tree stands tall and proud in the heart of the home, the adventure takes a creative turn. Untangling lights becomes a team effort as family members go through the bright mess to add a cozy, glittering glow to the tree. The room is bathed in a magical ambiance as the lights come to life, casting a gentle radiance that turns the simple decoration into a luminescent adventure.

Ornaments, each a vessel of memories and stories, become the protagonists in this festive tale. From cherished heirlooms passed down through generations to whimsical creations that reflect the latest trends, each bauble carries a unique narrative. The adventure in Christmas Tree Decorating is not merely about embellishing branches but about weaving a tapestry of family history, traditions, and the shared experiences that define the holiday season.

This joyful journey unleashes endless creative potential. Families engage in spirited debates over the placement of ornaments, contemplating the delicate balance between uniformity and delightful chaos. The youngest family members frequently take center stage, their joyful yells directing ornament placement and lending a comical element to the design. The adventure becomes a dynamic collaboration, an artistic expression that evolves with each new decoration.

The quest for the perfect tree topper is pivotal in the Christmas Tree Decorating adventure. Whether it's a classic star, an angel with outstretched wings, or a quirky creation that reflects the family's unique personality, the tree topper becomes the crowning glory. While searching for this symbolic ornament, family members share their thoughts and preferences, and the expedition culminates with the chosen topper being carefully positioned atop the tree.

The experience goes beyond the lights and sounds, including the culinary delights that characterize the holiday season. Fragrant pine needles mingle with the scent of cinnamon and the aroma of festive treats, creating an olfactory symphony that elevates the Christmas Tree Decorating experience. Now a vibrant centerpiece, the tree becomes a multisensory celebration that captivates both young and old, transporting them to a realm where the ordinary is enchanted and the season's spirit reigns supreme.

Stinging garlands and tinsel onto the tree becomes a playful expedition, a dance of shimmering strands that add a touch of glamour and merriment. The tree stands tall as a beacon of holiday cheer, transforming the space into a wintry wonderland. The adventure takes on a dynamic rhythm, a visual and tactile experience that unfolds with each layer of decoration, turning the tree into a work of art that captures the season's essence.

Social media becomes a virtual gallery where families proudly share snapshots of their Christmas Tree Decorating adventure. Hashtags such as #FestiveFamilyFun and #TreeTrimmingTraditions become digital markers of the collective joy emanating from homes worldwide. The journey reaches beyond private homes to form a worldwide community bound together by a common desire to experience holiday joy.

But there are humorous moments during the journey. Tangled strings of lights, playful debates over ornament placement, and the occasional toppled tree become part of the narrative. Instead of taking away from the magic, these setbacks give the experience a more genuine feel. Laughter becomes the season's soundtrack, echoing through the room as families navigate the challenges that arise during the Christmas Tree Decorating escapade.

In conclusion, Adventures in Christmas Tree Decorating is more than a decorative ritual; they are a joyous exploration of creativity, tradition, and the shared magic of the holiday season. From selecting the tree to untangling lights, from placing cherished ornaments to crowning the tree with a shimmering topper, each adventure step is imbued with a sense of wonder and togetherness. As families worldwide engage in this annual escapade, they create adorned trees and festive masterpieces that embody the season's spirit. This adventure turns the ordinary into the extraordinary and transforms homes into havens of holiday magic.

Stringing up the Twinkling Lights

The holiday season brings a magical transformation as neighborhoods, homes, and public spaces come alive with the warm glow of twinkling lights. The custom of hanging these sparkling ornaments has evolved into a global representation of happiness, celebration, and a sense of community. The simple sparkling lights are essential to illuminate our surroundings and add a magical touch as the days become shorter and the nights get longer.

The art of adorning spaces with twinkling lights has a rich history that spans cultures and centuries. Originating from the tradition of decorating Christmas trees in 16th-century Germany, the practice quickly gained popularity and spread throughout Europe. It wasn't long before twinkling lights became synonymous with the holiday season, transcending religious and cultural boundaries to become a global phenomenon.

One enchanting quality of twinkling lights is their ability to evoke nostalgia and create a sense of wonder. Just hanging these lights makes everyday rooms feel like magical places straight out of childhood dreams and treasured memories. Each twinkling morning becomes a beacon of warmth, drawing people together in a shared celebration of light and life.

Twinkling lights are more than just pretty; they have a deeper meaning. In a world often plagued by stress and strife, stringing up these lights is a collective endeavor to bring positivity and optimism. The process, undertaken alone or with loved ones, becomes a ritual that marks the beginning of a festive season filled with hope and goodwill.

As the holiday season approaches, individuals of all ages engage in the meticulous task of selecting, untangling, and arranging strings of lights. The variety of lamps available, from classic white to multicolored strands, allows for personalization, reflecting the unique tastes and preferences of those who partake in this annual tradition. The gentle glow emitted by these lights not only brightens physical spaces but also symbolizes the inner illumination accompanying the season of giving.

Communities, too, come alive with the collective effort to illuminate streets, parks, and public buildings. The synchronized display of twinkling lights in public spaces creates a shared experience that fosters a sense of unity and belonging. In cities worldwide, the unveiling of grand light displays marks the commencement of festive celebrations, drawing locals and visitors alike to witness the spectacle of lights dancing in harmony.

Beyond their role in seasonal festivities, twinkling lights have found a place in various cultural and religious celebrations, transcending their initial association with Christmas. During Diwali, the Hindu festival of lights, roadways are decked with colorful decorations, such as strings of lights that twinkle to represent the triumph of light over darkness. Similar to this, menorahs with lights attached are used by Jewish communities during Hanukkah to celebrate the wonder of one day's worth of oil lasting for eight days.

The allure of twinkling lights extends beyond their use in public spaces and festive decorations. Homes become canvases for personal expression as individuals infuse their living spaces with the warm radiance of these lights. Whether delicately framing windows, adorning mantels, or enveloping entire rooms, the arrangement of twinkling lights becomes a form of artistic expression that reflects the unique personality of each household.

The custom of hanging holiday lights has not been exempt from technological innovation. The introduction of LED technology has improved the energy efficiency, robustness, and versatility of lighting. The transition from traditional incandescent bulbs to LEDs has reduced environmental impact and allowed for more intricate and creative lighting displays. Intelligent lighting systems further enhance the experience, enabling users to control colors, patterns, and brightness with a simple tap on a smartphone.

While twinkling lights undoubtedly add a touch of magic to the holiday season, their impact extends beyond mere decoration. The psychological consequences of sunshine exposure have been the subject of several research, especially in the darker winter months. The soft glow of twinkling lights has been shown to positively impact mood, alleviating symptoms of seasonal affective disorder and creating a sense of coziness and comfort.

In conclusion, the tradition of stringing up twinkling lights represents more than just a decorative practice; it is a timeless ritual that brings people together, evokes nostalgia, and infuses spaces with a sense of magic and hope. Every year, as we start the chore of untangling strings and decorating our homes and neighborhoods with these shining jewels, we join in a communal celebration of light, happiness, and the feeling of community that characterizes the holiday season. Just hanging twinkling lights serves as a reminder that, even in the depths of darkness, the warmth and glow of shared festivities can brighten our lives and strengthen our bonds as a worldwide community.

When Ornaments Have Personalities

The holiday season invites us into a world of traditions and festivities, where every ornament hung on a tree becomes a storyteller, a memory holder, and, surprisingly, a bearer of personality. Ornaments can transcend their physical shapes and acquire unique characters, making them more than decorations. When families open boxes of treasured decorations every year, they take a trip down memory lane and rediscover the personality infused into these inanimate artifacts.

The custom of decorating trees with ornaments has a long history that dates back to ancient civilizations. However, it was in 16th-century Germany that the tradition of decorating Christmas trees took shape, marking the beginning of what would become a global phenomenon. Over the centuries, ornaments have evolved from simple fruits and nuts to intricate, handcrafted decorations. Yet, the personalization of these ornaments has elevated them from decorative items to cherished companions in the annual celebration of the holiday season.

One of the most enchanting aspects of ornaments with personalities is how they reflect the stories and experiences of the individuals or families who own them. Every ornament turns into a small, material time capsule that captures the spirit of a specific occasion or turning point. Whether a hand-painted bauble commemorating a child's first Christmas or a travel-themed ornament acquired during a memorable vacation, these tiny treasures tell tales that unfold with each passing holiday season.

The personality of an ornament is often intricately tied to the memories it holds. As families gather to trim the tree, unwrapping each ornament is akin to opening a chapter in a cherished storybook. The delicate glass ball from Grandma's collection may carry the whispered laughter of generations past, while the handmade ornament from a child's school project radiates the joy of youthful creativity. In this way, decorations become custodians of family narratives, preserving and retelling the stories that define us.

Furthermore, ornaments' personalities extend beyond only their outward manifestations. The emotions and sentiments associated with each ornament infuse them with a unique energy that can be felt when hung on the tree. A whimsical snowman ornament may evoke feelings of childlike wonder, while a vintage angel figurine may bring forth a sense of nostalgia. Choosing where to place each ornament on the tree becomes a deliberate and heartfelt decision as if arranging a cast of characters in a theatrical production.

Giving ornaments with particular themes or symbols as gifts has become a custom in certain families to show affection and shared interests. These thematic ornaments, such as those representing hobbies, professions, or significant life events, add a personalized touch to the tree. For instance, a musical note ornament may symbolize a family member's passion for music, while a tiny wedding bell commemorates a year of marital bliss. The precise act of choosing these ornaments with care adds layers to the story of the tree, assembling a picture of characters and experiences.

The personalities of ornaments extend beyond familial traditions and often spill into the realm of cultural and regional influences. In different parts of the world, specific ornaments may hold particular significance. Handmade decorations from foreign craftspeople, each with their own cultural tale, make their way into homes and weave a worldwide web of seasonal customs. The merging of these diverse ornaments on a single tree is a testament to the interconnectedness of humanity and the shared joy that transcends borders during the holiday season.

How ornaments convey personality has changed along with technological advancements. With the help of customization options like photo inserts and unique engravings, people can make ornaments that capture their tales. Digital decorations with lights and music add an interactive touch to the tree and accentuate the personalities they represent. These modern additions coexist harmoniously with traditional ornaments, demonstrating that the essence of holiday decorations lies not only in their form but also in the emotions and memories they carry.

In conclusion, ornaments with personalities transform from insignificant embellishments into traveling companions who accompany a person through history and customs. The tradition of hanging decorations on trees, where families gather annually to decorate them, goes beyond simple decoration. Each ornament is a vessel of memories, a conduit of emotions, and a storyteller with a unique personality. In the dance of twinkling lights and the shimmer of tinsel, the characters of these ornaments intertwine, creating a symphony of joy, nostalgia, and shared experiences that define the true spirit of the holiday season.

CHAPTER 6

Lights and Tinsel Tales

The Great Christmas Light Extravaganza

In the heart of winter, when the nights are the longest, and the air carries a crisp chill, communities worldwide come alive with the radiant glow of The Great Christmas Light Extravaganza. Every year, this custom—distinguished by a stunning display of festive lights—transforms regular neighborhoods into fantastical settings that enthrall and uplift everyone who sees them. The Great Christmas Light Extravaganza is more than a spectacle of twinkling bulbs and elaborate decorations; it is a communal celebration that transcends cultural and religious boundaries, uniting people in the shared joy of the holiday season.

The Great Christmas Light Extravaganza revolves around the long-standing custom of decorating buildings and public areas with spectacular and colorful light displays. As daylight wanes, the darkness is pushed back by the luminous brilliance of multicolored lights, creating a breathtaking panorama that captures the season's magic. The tradition traces its roots to decorating Christmas trees, which gained popularity in 17th-century Germany. Over the years, lighting candles on trees evolved into an elaborate art form extending beyond individual homes to entire streets, parks, and commercial districts.

The complex design of the Great Christmas Light Extravaganza is evidence of people's passion, inventiveness, and community. Homeowners put a lot of time, energy, and money into creating displays that can be simple and classy or wildly expensive. Elaborate light sculptures, animated figures, and synchronized light shows set to music contribute to the festive atmosphere, creating a visual symphony that resonates with the joyous spirit of the season. Occasionally, amicable neighborhood rivalries develop, motivating neighbors to surpass each other in producing the most amazing light show.

The transformative power of The Great Christmas Light Extravaganza extends beyond individual homes, as entire neighborhoods and communities become critical players in this collective celebration. Streets adorned with arches of twinkling lights and public spaces transformed into winter wonderlands become magnets for locals and visitors alike. The tradition fosters community as neighbors come together to share the joy of creating and experiencing these luminous displays. It is a time when the concept of "home" expands beyond individual residences to encompass the entire neighborhood, creating a sense of belonging and shared celebration.

The Great Christmas Light Extravaganza has a more profound meaning beyond its spectacular appearance, based on the spirit of charity and generosity. Many localities use the event to promote and increase donations to charity groups. In some instances, visitors are encouraged to make donations or contribute non-perishable goods for local charities as they enjoy the dazzling light displays. The tradition thus becomes a conduit for spreading generosity and kindness, emphasizing the importance of coming together to positively impact the lives of those less fortunate during the holiday season.

The impact of The Great Christmas Light Extravaganza extends beyond individual communities to regional and national levels. Official lighting ceremonies are a common way for cities and communities to usher in Christmas officially. These grand events, featuring celebrity performances, festive markets, and the ceremonious lighting of a towering Christmas tree, draw crowds and symbolize the unity and shared joy that define the season. The Great Christmas Light Extravaganza has become a beloved cultural event that attracts people of all backgrounds together.

The Great Christmas Light Extravaganza adopts distinctive cultural characteristics in some areas by fusing regional customs and themes with the light shows. For instance, cities with a solid cultural heritage can display light sculptures modeled after well-known art pieces, whereas coastal towns might use nautical motifs in their exhibits. This blending of tradition and innovation adds a layer of diversity to the celebration, making it a dynamic and inclusive experience that resonates with people of various backgrounds.

The Great Christmas Light Extravaganza has evolved significantly due to technological improvements. With their energy efficiency and vibrant colors, LED lights have become the preferred choice for many decorators, allowing for more elaborate and dynamic displays. Synchronized lighting systems, controlled by computer programs, enable homeowners and communities to choreograph intricate light shows set to music. The integration of intelligent technology has further enhanced the visitor experience, with some displays offering interactive elements that allow viewers to control aspects of the light show through their smartphones.

The Great Christmas Light Extravaganza's lasting appeal might be ascribed to its capacity to arouse nostalgia and amazement. Driving past neighborhoods decked out in holiday lights is a beloved yearly routine that brings back childhood memories for many. Families bundle up in warm layers, pile into cars, and embark on a magical journey through streets aglow with the spirit of the season. It is an everyday activity that unites people of all ages, forging enduring bonds and enhancing the enchantment that characterizes the holiday season.

To sum up, The Great Christmas Light Extravaganza is a custom that involves more than just decorating spaces with holiday lights. It's a collective celebration that turns streets into glowing canvases and brings people together to share the joy of the holidays. The elaborate displays, the sense of community, and the charitable initiatives associated with this tradition encapsulate the spirit of giving, togetherness, and wonder that defines the holiday season. As we marvel at the twinkling lights and festive displays, we are reminded that, in the darkest of nights, the collective brilliance of communities coming together can illuminate the world with the light of joy and celebration.

A Sparkling Comedy

In the grand tapestry of holiday traditions, one often-overlooked star takes center stage, quite literally, in the perennial spectacle of decorating – the humble yet glittering tinsel. Its capacity to elevate the commonplace to the extraordinary Tinsel has become integral to the festive season, adorning trees, homes, and public spaces with its shimmering allure. Beyond its decorative role, tinsel has a history that sparkles with nostalgia, humor, and a touch of whimsy, making it a key player in the comedy of holiday festivities.

The origins of tinsel trace back to 17th-century Germany, which was initially made from strands of real silver. But as tinsel's appeal increased, so did the demand for a more readily available and reasonably priced substitute. By the 20th century, the modern incarnation of glitz emerged, consisting of lightweight, metallic strands that captured and reflected light, creating a dazzling effect. These days, tinsel is available in various colors and materials, ranging from traditional silver and gold to vivid shades that suit specific preferences and design ideas.

The role of tinsel in holiday decorating is not merely aesthetic; it contributes to the visual symphony that defines the festive season. When carefully draped on Christmas trees, tinsel adds a touch of the supernatural, turning evergreen branches into radiant cascades of light. Its reflective properties create a dynamic interplay with twinkling lights, enhancing the overall brilliance of the holiday display. Tinsel's ability to catch and reflect light gives it a unique quality, transforming static decorations into dynamic elements that dance and shimmer in the glow of festive illumination.

However, tinsel's role in the holiday comedy is not limited to its visual impact; it is also deeply intertwined with the art of decorating itself. The yearly custom of decorating Christmas trees with tinsel frequently requires a balance between accuracy and creativity. The difficulty is not only in uniformly arranging the glitz but also in striking that fine line between extravagance and moderation. Every strand is placed as if it were a dance, a ballet of glitter and shine that turns the tree into a magnificent work of holiday art.

Yet, the comedy of tinsel unfolds amid this seemingly meticulous process. Tinsel has a mischievous nature, and as anyone who has engaged in decorating knows, it tends to cling to everything except the tree branches. Fingers, clothing, pets, and unsuspecting family members become unwitting victims of the tinsel tumult as the sparkling strands seem to possess a life of their own. The delicate task of draping tinsel becomes a whimsical affair, with laughter and good-natured banter filling the air as individuals navigate the challenges posed by this festive adornment.

Tinsel's comic abilities transcend the house to public areas and storefront displays. The meticulous arrangement of tinsel in store windows, city streets, and public squares becomes a theatrical production, with each strand playing a role in the larger drama of holiday decoration. The festive mood of joy and celebration that permeates the Christmas season is enhanced by tinsel's ability to draw the eye and exude luxury. It enables visitors to fully immerse themselves in the festivities by transforming everyday areas into magical worlds.

Although tinsel adds glitz and humor to the holidays, it is not without controversy. Some purists contend that tinsel takes away from the Christmas tree's inherent beauty, comparing it to a diversion that masks the grace of the evergreen limbs. The debate over whether to embrace the glimmering allure of tinsel or opt for a more minimalistic approach is a recurring theme in discussions about holiday decorating. However, for many, tinsel is not just about aesthetics but about embracing the whimsy, nostalgia, and lightheartedness that define the season's spirit.

The festive comedy's use of tinsel is further highlighted by its nostalgic connotations. For generations, tinsel has been a staple in holiday decorating, evoking memories of childhood wonder and the season's magic. Unwrapping a box of tinsel and hanging it from the tree develops into a custom that bridges the present and recollections of previous holidays. Tinsel becomes a tangible link to the traditions of yesteryear, carrying with it the laughter, joy, and perhaps a few comical mishaps that have become part of the family lore.

Tinsels have been used as decorations and influenced popular culture, appearing as a representation of joyousness in music, movies, and literature. The sparkling allure of tinsel has been immortalized in holiday songs that celebrate the season's magic, and its presence in festive films often adds a touch of whimsy to the cinematic landscape. Tinsel becomes more than a decorative element; it is a cultural icon that embodies the spirit of merriment and celebration, appearing in everything from classic holiday films to modern animated favorites.

Technology development has also been aided by developments in tinsel, with innovations such as holographic tinsel and LED-lit strands offering new dimensions to its festive charm. These contemporary modifications give conventional décor a fresh look and give decorators even more ways to showcase their inventiveness. The incorporation of technology into tinsel not only enhances its visual impact but ensures that it remains a relevant and dynamic part of holiday decorating for generations to come.

In conclusion, with its sparkling comedy, tinsel has earned its place as an iconic element of holiday celebrations. Its ability to transform ordinary spaces into enchanting realms and mischievous nature and nostalgic charm make tinsel a beloved and enduring tradition. As we engage in the annual ritual of adorning our homes with these glittering strands, we participate in the grand comedy of holiday decorating. A festive mood that goes beyond decoration to become a celebration of joy, camaraderie, and the timeless enchantment of the Christmas season is created by the interplay of laughter, memories, and the shimmering appeal of tinsel.

Decorating the House with Holiday Hilarity

The holiday season heralds a time of warmth, joy, and the age-old tradition of transforming our living spaces into festive wonderlands. Decorating the house becomes a family tradition filled with pleasure, cherished memories, and a dash of seasonal humor as families open boxes of decorations and untangle strings of lights. Beyond embellishing our homes, decorating for the holidays is a whimsical journey that unfolds with a unique blend of creativity and lightheartedness.

The centerpiece of holiday decorating is often the Christmas tree—a symbol that transcends religious and cultural boundaries. The process of selecting, transporting, and positioning the tree within the home is an adventure filled with moments of hilarity. Families embark on excursions to tree farms, embracing the crisp winter air and the challenge of finding the perfect specimen. The quest for the "ideal" tree is often accompanied by laughter as family members debate the merits of various candidates, from the perfectly symmetrical to the charmingly asymmetrical. The comical sight of families negotiating the logistics of strapping a tree to the roof of a car or navigating narrow doorways adds an element of slapstick humor to the holiday tradition.

The real fun starts when a treasure trove of decorations is unwrapped once the tree is firmly in place. The ornament collection, accumulated over years and generations, is a testament to the evolving tastes and personalities of the family. Each ornament is a tiny time capsule, carrying with it the stories of holidays past. As you peel back the layers of these fragile souvenirs, you'll undoubtedly hear about past encounters, reminiscences, and forgotten favorites. The tree takes on a life of its own as ornaments are thoughtfully strung from branches, embellished with memories, characters, and a hint of Christmas humor.

With their sparkling allure, lights play a crucial role in turning the tree into a magical focal point. The untangling of strands, the occasional malfunctioning bulb, and the collaborative effort to distribute the lights evenly create opportunities for laughter and camaraderie. The interplay of colors and the dance of lights bring the tree to life, transforming it from a simple evergreen into a luminous spectacle that radiates the festive spirit. Decorating with lights becomes a group activity that promotes the happiness and coziness of the holiday season.

The mantle, often considered the heart of the home, becomes a canvas for holiday creativity. When thoughtfully hung, stockings become not simply containers for tiny gifts but a fun way to add a playful touch of customization. The careful arrangement of figurines, candles, and greenery on the mantle becomes an art form, blending aesthetic appeal with a touch of whimsy. Decorating the cover often involves a humorous negotiation of space as family members compete for the most prominent display spots for their favorite decorations. The mantle, adorned with holiday charm, becomes a focal point for laughter and storytelling.

Wreaths, garlands, and other festive elements find their way into various nooks and crannies of the home, adding layers of holiday cheer. The house's façade also serves as a blank canvas for artistic interpretation. The hanging of outdoor lights, the inflating of whimsical holiday characters on the lawn, and the occasional mishap with unruly inflatable decorations all contribute to the holiday hilarity. The exterior transformation is a community affair, with neighbors exchanging smiles and good-natured banter as they embark on their decorating adventures. In this communal effort, the neighborhood becomes a stage for shared laughter and a testament to the collective spirit of the season.

The kitchen, a hub of activity throughout the year, plays a unique role during the holidays. Baking and decorating gingerbread cookies, crafting edible ornaments, and experimenting with festive recipes become opportunities for culinary creativity and joy. The sweet aroma of holiday treats fills the air as families gather in the kitchen, donning festive aprons and engaging in friendly competitions to create the most elaborate gingerbread house. The culinary escapades are not just about creating delectable delights; they celebrate the joyous chaos that defines holiday gatherings.

The hanging of stockings is a practice that is inextricably linked to centuries-old mythology. Filling stockings with small surprises and treats is a source of amusement for both the givers and receivers. The thoughtful arrangement of socks, frequently coupled with jovial conjecture on their contents, contributes a sense of excitement and joy to the seasonal celebrations. Discovering unique and humorous stocking stuffers becomes a fun game, with every tiny thing adding a dash of festive humor.

Holiday decorating is not without its share of comical mishaps. The precarious balancing act of standing on chairs to reach high shelves, the inevitable entanglement in strings of lights, and the occasional toppling of a carefully arranged display all contribute to the laughter-filled narrative of holiday preparations. These hilarious incidents serve as the connecting threads in the Christmas memory tapestry, spinning tales that are laughed about and relived for years.

The usage of electronics in contemporary Christmas décor opens up new entertainment possibilities. Smart home devices allow synchronized light shows, automated decorations, and even voice-activated holiday displays. Technology integration adds a contemporary twist to the age-old tradition, providing opportunities for families to explore the intersection of innovation and festive creativity. The juxtaposition of traditional decorations with modern technological marvels creates a harmonious blend of nostalgia and progress in the holiday decorating narrative.

In conclusion, holiday home décor is a vibrant, humorous trip that unites families and communities rather than just being a beautiful project. From selecting the perfect tree to the creative arrangement of ornaments, lights, and decorations, each step is infused with camaraderie, nostalgia, and holiday hilarity. As we deck the halls, trim the tree, and transform our living spaces into festive retreats, we are not just creating a visual spectacle; we are participating in a cherished tradition that encapsulates the magic, joy, and shared laughter of the holiday season.

CHAPTER 7

Snowman Jokes and
Icy Chuckles

Snowman Stand-Up

In the whimsical world of holiday decorations, a perennial favorite brings charm and joy to the winter landscape—the snowman. Beyond its traditional role as a symbol of winter and holiday cheer, the snowman takes on a dynamic persona in the concept of "Snowman Stand-Up." This delightful twist on the classic snowman tradition transforms these frosty figures into comical characters, each with a unique personality and a penchant for bringing laughter to the season.

Creating a snowman has long been a cherished winter pastime, with families and friends joining forces to roll, stack, and sculpt snow into a whimsical figure. Making a snowman becomes a group activity where everyone adds their creative touch to the finished product. However, the idea of Snowman Stand-Up brings a new level of humor to this age-old custom. As the snow takes shape and the snowman comes to life, its appearance takes on the characteristics of a stand-up comedian, complete with distinct features that suggest a lighthearted and pleasant demeanor.

The face of a Snowman Stand-Up is a canvas for creativity, featuring a carrot for a nose, coal for eyes and mouth, and perhaps a jaunty top hat or scarf to complete the ensemble. The arrangement of these features is not merely a decorative task; it is an art form that imbues the snowman with its unique personality. Adding accessories like eyeglasses, a pipe, or an oddball look enhances the snowman's humorous persona. It makes it appear as though it is ready to perform a stand-up performance with a winter theme.

Snowman Stand-Up is wider than the traditional trio of snowballs stacked atop one another. This quirky version allows snowmen to assume many shapes and positions, each suggesting a different humorous scenario. Whether it's a snowman mid-dance, sporting an air of theatrical elegance, or a laid-back snowman soaking up winter sun with a beach chair and sunglasses, each creation becomes a miniature work of art that tells a humorous tale. The arrangement of snowmen in creative tableaus further enhances the comedic narrative, turning a snowy landscape into a frosty comedy club.

The humor in Snowman Stand-Up extends beyond the physical appearance of these frosty jesters. It frequently entails the deft integration of accessories and objects that heighten the mood. Snowmen may find themselves amid a snowball fight, armed with tiny snowball projectiles, or be surrounded by miniature snow angels basking in their comedic brilliance. The only restrictions on the settings are your imagination and the end product is a group of snowmen having fun and making people smile and laugh.

Communities worldwide have embraced the spirit of Snowman Stand-Up, turning public spaces into whimsical winter wonderlands. Snowman festivals and competitions encourage participants to unleash their creativity and humor as they craft larger-than-life snowmen with eye-catching personalities. Both locals and visitors are drawn to these gatherings, which promote a feeling of camaraderie and mutual happiness as people take in the inventive and frequently humorous snowman constructions. From the traditional to the avant-garde, the snowmen on display become a testament to the boundless creativity that winter's frozen canvas inspires.

Snowman Stand-Up is charming because of its aesthetic appeal and because it may be used as an idea for holiday stories and celebrations. Some communities organize snowman-themed events, including snowman-building contests, where participants compete to create the most humorous and imaginative snowman. These contests become opportunities for friendly rivalry, with participants showcasing their wit and creativity through the snow. The result is a landscape dotted with snowmen that reflect the community's collective sense of humor and originality.

Snowman Stand-Up has also found a home in popular culture, appearing in holiday movies, cartoons, and literature. Animated snowmen, brought to life with mischievous expressions and humorous antics, have become beloved characters in the pantheon of holiday storytelling. These wacky depictions of snowmen bring a little humor to the season, resulting in charming and enduring moments that appeal to viewers of all ages. The appeal of these snowmen lies not just in their visual charm but in the laughter and joy they bring to the hearts of those who encounter them.

The tradition of Snowman Stand-Up is not without its challenges. Crafting snowmen relies heavily on the cooperation of weather conditions, and the availability of suitable snow is only sometimes guaranteed. Creative alternatives, such as inflatable or artificial snowmen, play in regions with sparse snowfall. While these substitutes lack the ephemeral charm of natural snow, they offer an opportunity for individuals in snow-deprived areas to partake in the festive fun and contribute their humorous interpretations to the snowman tradition.

 For instance, the fabrication of lit snowmen that come to life in the nighttime scenery is made possible by outdoor lighting. Solar-powered or LED lights embedded within the snowman's design add a magical glow to these frosty figures, turning them into luminous comedians that delight passersby. The creative possibilities are increased by the incorporation of technology, creating dynamic and interactive snowman displays that enthrall viewers with their brilliant festiveness.

In conclusion, Snowman Stand-Up is more than just a charming winter tradition; it is a celebration of creativity, humor, and the joyous spirit of the holiday season. The lighthearted personalities of these frosty comedians, whether crafted in backyards or showcased in public spaces, bring a touch of whimsy to the winter landscape.

Participating in the lighthearted art form of Snowman Stand-Up allows groups and people to add to a shared story that blends humor, imagination, and the season's beauty into the theme of winter celebrations.

Snowball Fights and Friendly Pranks

A timeless and vibrant tradition comes to life in the middle of winter, when everything is completely covered in a perfect layer of white: the joyful art of snowball battles and amusing pranks. Children and adults enjoy this ancient custom, which turns winter into a time for playfulness, laughing, and companionship. From spontaneous snowball battles to carefully orchestrated pranks, the tradition embodies the lighthearted essence of the colder months, fostering a sense of community and shared joy.

The base of this winter activity is the plenty of snow, which provides both a canvas and ammo for the subsequent intense exchanges. Snowball fights are a universal winter language, transcending cultural and geographical boundaries. Just thinking of a snowball fight brings back happy childhood memories, the snappy bite of chilly air, and the excitement of friendly rivalry. As the first snowfall blankets neighborhoods, parks, and schoolyards, the stage is set for impromptu skirmishes that bring people of all ages together in the exhilarating dance of snowball warfare.

The beauty of a snowball fight lies in its simplicity—a shared understanding that the snowy battlefield is a canvas for camaraderie rather than aggression. Building forts, making snowballs, and fighting spiritedly break down barriers and promote solidarity among friends, family, and strangers. The laughter that rings out amid the flurry of snowflakes becomes a testament to the joyous camaraderie that arises from the shared experience of a well-fought snowball skirmish.

Children, in particular, embrace the magic of snowball fights with unbridled enthusiasm. Creating the ideal snowball becomes a talent that must be developed, and the snow-covered terrain becomes an infinitely creative playground. The giggles and shrieks of delight as children duck, dodge, and launch snowballs at one another create a symphony of winter joy that resonates with the timeless spirit of the season. Friendships are made, and memories are inscribed in the hearts of individuals who engage in these lighthearted conflicts.

While snowball fights are spontaneous and joyous, the tradition of friendly jokes adds an element of mischief and surprise to the winter landscape. From the classic snowball sneak attack to more elaborate schemes, the art of winter pranking transforms snowy settings into theaters of amusement. The mischievous spirit of winter pranks fosters a sense of camaraderie among participants, who share in the laughter and good-natured mischief that defines the season.

Snowmen, often considered the benign ambassadors of winter, become unwitting accomplices in the theater of friendly pranks. The strategic placement of snowballs in the clutches of a snowman, the addition of whimsical accessories, or the clever arrangement of snowmen in humorous tableaus become opportunities for creative winter mischief. Passersby are greeted not just by the sight of traditional snowmen but by unexpected and comical scenes that add a whimsy to the winter landscape.

Good-natured snowball gags frequently transcend the backyard and enter the world of formal gatherings. Snowball festivals, where participants gather to orchestrate snowball battles, have become popular community traditions in various regions. These events, marked by teams, strategies, and good-natured competition, bring together people of all ages to revel in the camaraderie and joy of a shared winter adventure. These snowball celebrations' joyous ambiance perfectly encapsulates the feeling of togetherness, playfulness, and shared laughter that characterizes the winter season.

Winter jokes are also played at work when coworkers take advantage of the chance to lighten the mood and have fun during the chilly months. The workplace becomes a canvas for good-natured winter mischief, from surprise snowball barrages during lunch breaks to creative office pranks involving snowmen or winter-themed decorations. These lighthearted gestures serve as a welcome respite from the daily grind, fostering a sense of camaraderie and shared joy among colleagues.

While the tradition of snowball fights and friendly pranks embodies the spirit of playfulness, it is not without its considerations. The word "friendly" must be emphasized because the goal is to foster a sense of joy and togetherness among all participants rather than to injure or cause suffering. By acknowledging the value of mutual enjoyment and consent, participants ensure that the winter celebrations remain a place of joy and camaraderie rather than discomfort or conflict.

In a world where the pace of life often feels frenetic, the tradition of snowball fights and friendly pranks reminds us of the value of slowing down, embracing spontaneity, and fostering connections with those around us. The laughter that arises from the joyous chaos of a snowball fight or the surprise of a well-executed winter prank creates moments of shared joy that bridge generations and cultivate a sense of community.

Technology has also evolved into a fun partner in the custom of winter mischief. Social media platforms become showcases for the creativity of snowball fights and pranks, with participants sharing photos and videos of their wintry escapades. The virtual realm extends the reach of these lighthearted traditions, allowing individuals to connect and share in the laughter across geographical distances. The digital landscape becomes a gallery of winter joy, capturing the spirit of snowball fights and friendly pranks for a global audience.

In conclusion, snowball fights and friendly pranks are not just whimsical winter traditions but timeless expressions of joy, camaraderie, and playfulness. From impromptu snowball battles that turn snow-covered landscapes into arenas of laughter to the creative mischief of winter pranks that add a touch of whimsy to the season, these traditions transcend age, culture, and geography. As we engage in the spirited dance of snowball fights and friendly pranks, we embrace the magic of winter, forging connections, creating memories, and reveling in the shared joy that defines the heartwarming tradition of playful winter mischief.

Snow Angels with a Sense of Humor

In the quiet hush of freshly fallen snow, a whimsical tradition comes to life—the creation of snow angels. Humor adds a fresh depth to this traditional winter activity, which is frequently connected to purity and simplicity. Snow angels, with a playful twist, become not just imprints in the snow but characters with personality, charm, and a touch of comedic flair. As individuals, young and old, venture into the winter wonderland to create these iconic figures, the tradition of making snow angels becomes a delightful expression of creativity, humor, and the timeless joy that winter brings.

An essential imprint created by laying down and moving one's arms and legs in tandem to create a symmetrical design reminiscent of angelic wings is the traditional snow angel. But the idea behind Snow Angels with a Sense of Humor infuses this ancient custom with a delicious dash of inventiveness and fun. Rather than adhering strictly to the conventional form, individuals embrace the opportunity to inject personality and amusement into their snowy counterparts.

The canvas for Snow Angels with a Sense of Humor extends beyond the backyard and into public spaces, parks, and even urban landscapes. The once-serene fields of snow transform into canvases for playful expression, with snow angels adopting quirky poses, whimsical accessories, and even facial expressions that suggest a lighthearted personality. A snow angel with raised eyebrows or a sly smile becomes not just a random imprint but a character that engages the imagination and elicits smiles from those who encounter it.

With their boundless creativity and natural inclination for playfulness, children often take the lead in infusing humor into the tradition of snow angels. Lying down in the snow becomes an opportunity for self-expression, as young imaginations run wild with ideas of snow angels engaged in comical antics, sporting imaginary accessories, or even appearing to engage in a conversation with nearby snowmen. The pure satisfaction of using the winter landscape as a blank canvas for entertainment is demonstrated by the laughing that follows these artistic endeavors.

As winter festivals and community events embrace the notion of Snow Angels with a Sense of Humor, public spaces become arenas for creative expression. Snow angel contests, in which competitors compete to earn the title of most creative or humorous snow angel, attract large audiences and turn public areas into exhibitions of inventive winter architecture. Making snow angels becomes more than a solo project; it becomes a group activity where people add special touches to the custom and spread happiness among themselves.

Incorporating a sense of humor into snow angels often involves the addition of accessories and props that elevate the notion to new heights. Snow angels adorned with makeshift hats, scarves, and even sunglasses become characters with distinct personalities. Using objects in the surrounding environment, such as twigs for arms or pinecones for eyes, adds a touch of natural charm to these playful creations. The careful arrangement of these accessories becomes an art form, turning each snow angel into a miniature sculpture that tells a lighthearted story.

The custom of Snow Angels with a Sense of Humor transcends daytime hours into the enchanted world of winter evenings. Illuminated snow angels, created by strategically placing lights within the snow, add a captivating glow to the winter landscape. These luminous figures become ethereal beings that dance in the moonlight, capturing the imagination and infusing the nighttime winter scene with a sense of wonder. Snow angels are transformed into bright spirits by the contrast of light and comedy, captivating anyone outside into the cold winter air.

The innovative potential of Snow Angels with a Sense of Humor is further enhanced by integrating technology. Drones with cameras capture aerial views of elaborate snow angel designs, allowing individuals to share their creations with a broader audience. Social media becomes a platform for showcasing the creativity and humor of snow angels, turning these winter characters into viral sensations that bring smiles to people worldwide. The digital landscape becomes a gallery of winter whimsy, with individuals sharing their unique interpretations of the classic snow angel tradition.

Making Snow Angels with a Sense of Humor is more than just a pretty picture; it has more profound meaning. It's a celebration of the fun attitude that characterizes the winter months—a reminder that there are opportunities for happiness and creativity even amid the chill and frost. The laughter accompanying the creation of these comical snow angels becomes a balm for the winter blues, lifting spirits and fostering a sense of community among those who partake in the tradition.

In conclusion, Snow Angels with a Sense of Humor breathes new life into the timeless tradition of creating imprints in the snow. What used to be a straightforward exercise of lying down and coordinating limb movements becomes a blank canvas for imagination, creativity, and fun. Whether crafted by children in backyard escapades, showcased in community events, or shared with the world through technology, these snow angels capture the essence of winter joy with a humorous twist. As young and old individuals venture into the snowy landscape to create these comical figures, they contribute to a collective celebration of winter as a season not just of cold and frost but of laughter, creativity, and the timeless magic of Snow Angels with a Sense of Humor.

CHAPTER 8

Snowball Fights and
Snow Angels

Epic Snowball Fight Chronicles

In the heart of winter, when the world is blanketed in a pristine layer of snow, a tradition as timeless as the season itself comes to life—the epic snowball fight. Far more than a spontaneous burst of wintertime joy, these battles are the stuff of legends, etching indelible memories into the hearts of participants and spectators alike. The Epic Snowball Fight Chronicles weave a tale of camaraderie, strategic planning, and sheer exhilaration as friends, families, and even entire communities engage in spirited battles that transcend the simple act of throwing snow.

The epic snowball fight is an age-old tradition that transforms ordinary winter days into memorable adventures. As the first snowfall graces the landscape, a silent pact emerges among those eager to partake in this annual ritual. The construction of forts and stockpiling of snowballs become strategic maneuvers, executed with a level of planning and precision that rivals military campaigns. What starts as a fun project turns into a large-scale event where players dress in homemade armor, craft snowball ammo, and scout the area for the best viewing spots.

With their boundless energy and natural inclination for play, children often take the lead in organizing epic snowball fights. Backyards turn into battlegrounds, and snow-covered terrain becomes enormous arenas for friendly skirmishes. The laughter accompanying the construction of forts and the launch of the first snowball creates a symphony of joy that echoes through neighborhoods. As friends and siblings gather in the snowy expanse, alliances are formed, battle strategies are devised, and the stage is set for an epic clash of snowbound titans.

Yet, the epic snowball fight is not limited to childhood; it is a tradition that transcends age, bringing together people from all walks of life. Families engage in intergenerational battles, with parents and grandparents joining the fray alongside the younger generation. The shared experience of crafting snowballs, constructing forts, and engaging in spirited combat creates bonds that bridge generational divides. In these moments of snowy camaraderie, participants become not just players in a winter game but contributors to a collective narrative that spans years and generations.

Communities, too, embrace the spirit of the epic snowball fight, organizing large-scale events that draw participants from far and wide. Snowball festivals and competitions become winter traditions, featuring teams, elaborate fortresses, and strategic snowball weaponry. The communal atmosphere that permeates these events fosters a sense of shared joy as neighbors and strangers come together to revel in the thrill of friendly competition and the magic of winter.

The strategic aspect of the epic snowball fight cannot be overstated. Participants refine their abilities, learning to build the ideal snowball, bolster their defenses, and deliver pinpoint attacks. The snow-covered landscape becomes a canvas for creative tactics, with participants utilizing natural features such as trees and mounds of snow for cover. The ebb and flow of battle, marked by laughter, shouts, and the occasional snowball ambush, transform the winter terrain into a dynamic arena where participants engage in a dance of strategy and skill.

Amid the epic snowball fight, camaraderie prevails even as participants find themselves on opposing sides. The shared experience of navigating the challenges of snow-covered terrain, the thrill of a well-aimed snowball, and the joy of friendly competition create a bond that transcends the temporary alliances formed during the battle. Whether engaged in a friendly skirmish with neighbors or participating in a large-scale community event, participants find themselves connected by the shared laughter and exhilaration that defines the epic snowball fight.

The tradition of epic snowball fights has its rules and rituals. The crafting of the first snowball, the strategic placement of forts, and the ceremonial countdown before the first volley add to the anticipation and excitement. Participants often come adorned in layers of winter gear, transforming the battlefield into a colorful array of scarves, hats, and snowsuits. The winter attire becomes a practical necessity and a symbol of participation in a time-honored tradition that celebrates the season's joy.

Epic snowball fights also became popular and immortalized in literature, film, and art. The iconic image of snowball fights, captured in paintings and depicted in holiday movies, evokes a sense of nostalgia and merriment. These cultural representations serve as a testament to the enduring appeal of the epic snowball fight, capturing the imagination and hearts of worldwide audiences.

The aftermath of an epic snowball fight is marked by more than just the physical remnants of snow forts and scattered ammunition. It is a moment of shared triumph and camaraderie, with participants relishing the memories of strategic victories, daring escapes, and the joyous chaos that defines the battle. Wet mittens, rosy cheeks, and snow-covered clothing become badges of honor, worn with pride as a testament to the winter adventure that unfolded.

The epic snowball fight has found new ways to be expressed as technology develops. Virtual reality simulations and online gaming platforms allow individuals to experience the thrill of a snowball fight from the comfort of their homes, connecting with friends and fellow enthusiasts across the globe. While these digital iterations capture the essence of winter fun, they also underscore the enduring appeal of the traditional, real-world epic snowball fight—the tactile experience, the joy of physical exertion, and the shared laughter from engaging with the elements.

In conclusion, the Epic Snowball Fight Chronicles capture the spirit of winter in a tale of camaraderie, strategy, and unbridled joy. From impromptu backyard skirmishes to organized community events, the tradition of the epic snowball fight weaves a narrative that transcends age, bringing people together in the shared celebration of winter. As friends, families, and communities engage in these spirited battles, they contribute to a collective story that spans generations, forging bonds and creating memories that endure long after the snow has melted.

Mastering the Art of Snow Angels

In the serene landscape of winter, when the world is transformed into a canvas of glistening white, a time-honored tradition takes center stage—the creation of snow angels. This seemingly straightforward gesture—lying down in the snow and gently moving one's arms and legs to make an ethereal imprint—is much more than just a fanciful way to celebrate winter. Learning to create snow angels is a skill that calls for talent, imagination, and respect for the fleeting beauty of the season.

At its core, the creation of a snow angel is a celebration of winter's pure and simple pleasures. The canvas, a duvet of just-fallen snow, invites people to connect with nature. The act of lying down in the snow is a deliberate surrender to the serene beauty of winter, an invitation to become one with the landscape and leave behind a trace of one's presence in a simple and profound form.

Yet, mastering the art of snow angels goes beyond the basic mechanics of the motion. It requires an awareness of the surroundings and an artistic spirit that turns the act into a unique way for the performer to show happiness and playfulness. Children, with their boundless imaginations, often lead the way in infusing this winter tradition with a sense of wonder. The choice of accessories, such as scarves, hats, or even twigs for arms, becomes a form of artistic expression, turning the snow angel into a miniature sculpture that reflects the unique personality of its creator.

The artistry of snow angels extends beyond the individual imprint to the creation of intricate patterns and scenes. Families and friends, gathering in snow-covered landscapes, often collaborate to craft larger-than-life snow angels that form a collective masterpiece. The snow becomes a medium for creativity, and the landscape transforms into a gallery of angelic forms that tell a collective story of shared joy and connection.

The magic of mastering the art of snow angels lies in the creative potential inherent in the winter landscape. A snowy canvas is a flat surface and a three-dimensional expanse of possibilities. Those who engage in the tradition of snow angels often embrace the surrounding environment, utilizing natural features such as mounds of snow or elevated terrain to enhance the design. The end effect is not merely an imprint but a tasteful blending of the unique form with the natural curves of the wintry surroundings.

With their inherent sense of playfulness, children often imbue the snow angel with a sense of character. The imprint becomes more than just a silhouette; it represents an imaginary friend or a winter spirit. Children may add accessories such as rocks for eyes or twigs for arms, creating a whimsical snow companion that embodies the essence of winter play. In this way, mastering the art of snow angels becomes a form of storytelling where each imprint carries a unique narrative.

People of many ages participate in the custom of making snow angels, which transcends childish whimsy. Even adults can find happiness and comfort in lying in the snow and letting the peaceful beauty of winter surround them. For some, the creation of snow angels becomes a form of meditation—a moment of connection with nature that provides a respite from the demands of daily life. People discover renewal in these silent moments and an ageless feeling of awe.

Communities often come together to celebrate the art of snow angels through organized events and festivals. Snow angel contests, in which competitors compete for the most intricate or imaginative design title, attract large crowds and foster a joyous mood. The winter landscape becomes a stage for artistic expression, with individuals and teams collaborating to craft intricate patterns, scenes, and even messages in the snow. These communal events foster a sense of shared joy, turning the creation of snow angels into a collective celebration of winter's enchanting beauty.

As technology advances, the art of snow angels finds new expressions in the digital realm. Virtual reality experiences and augmented reality apps allow individuals to create virtual snow angels in the comfort of their homes, blending the nostalgia of a winter tradition with the innovations of the digital age. While these virtual iterations capture the essence of snow angel creation, they also underscore the enduring appeal of the tactile, real-world experience—a connection with the elements and a celebration of the sensory delights of winter.

The temporary nature of snow angels adds to their allure. Unlike traditional art forms that endure over time, snow angels are transient, subject to the whims of temperature and weather conditions. The impermanence of these creations enhances their beauty, turning each snow angel into a fleeting masterpiece that exists briefly before melting into the winter landscape. This transient state serves as a reminder of how valuable and quick the winter season is.

In conclusion, mastering the art of snow angels is not just about creating imprints in the snow; it is a celebration of creativity, playfulness, and the enchanting beauty of winter. From the simple joy of lying down in the snow to the collaborative efforts of families and communities, the tradition of snow angels captures the magic of the season. As individuals, young and old, venture into snow-covered landscapes to create these ethereal imprints, they contribute to a timeless narrative that weaves together the beauty of winter, the joy of play, and the enduring enchantment of mastering the art of snow angels.

When Snowmen Join the Battle

In the enchanting landscape of winter, where the world is blanketed in a pristine coat of snow, a time-honored tradition takes a whimsical turn—the arrival of snowmen on the battlefield. Beyond their traditional role as benign winter ambassadors, snowmen, when infused with a playful spirit, transform into formidable allies in the epic battles that define the season. The idea behind "When Snowmen Join the Battle" infuses the winter scene with enchantment and mischief, transforming these icy characters into essential participants in the long-standing custom of snowball battles, amicable skirmishes, and comrades and opponents.

The creation of snowmen is a cherished winter pastime, with families and friends coming together to sculpt and adorn these frozen companions. Yet, the idea of snowmen joining the battle introduces an element of creative storytelling and imaginative play that elevates the tradition to new heights. The snowmen, once mere onlookers in the winter landscape, become active participants, each with its unique personality and role in the snowy skirmishes that unfold.

The notion of snowmen joining the battle begins with the careful construction of these frozen allies. From the classic three-tiered snowman with coal eyes and a carrot nose to more elaborate and imaginative designs, each snowman becomes a character in the unfolding winter narrative. The choice of accessories, such as hats, scarves, and even miniature props, contributes to the snowman's personality, suggesting a readiness to join the snowy fray.

Snowmen are strategically placed on the battlefield, ranging from defenders of snow forts to instigators of friendly mischief. With a wicked glint in their coal eyes, some snowmen brandish snowball ammunition, ready to fire a frozen missile at unsuspecting attendees. Others may find themselves perched atop snow forts, overseeing the battlefield with a regal air, while a carefree snowman might be caught mid-dance, adding a touch of fun to the wintry clash.

The act of snowmen joining the battle is not limited to backyard skirmishes; it extends into organized events and community festivals. Snowman-building competitions take on a new dimension, with participants challenged to craft visually appealing snowmen and imbue them with a sense of character and humor. Judges and spectators alike are treated to a winter spectacle as snowmen with distinct personalities take center stage, becoming integral players in the lively competitions celebrating the art of winter play.

The humor of snowmen joining the battle extends beyond their physical appearance to the clever incorporation of props and accessories. Snowmen may find themselves armed with miniature snowball catapults, ready to launch frozen projectiles. Some may sport sunglasses and scarves, adopting a calm demeanor as they navigate the snowy landscape. The imaginative use of accessories turns snowmen into animated characters, suggesting a lively presence that adds an extra layer of amusement to the winter tableau.

The concept of snowmen joining the battle has found its way into popular culture, making appearances in holiday movies, cartoons, and literature. Animated snowmen, brought to life with mischievous expressions and humorous antics, have become beloved characters in the winter storytelling tradition. These wacky depictions of snowmen bring a little humor to the season, resulting in charming and enduring moments that appeal to viewers of all ages. The appeal of these snowmen lies not just in their visual charm but in the laughter and joy they bring to the hearts of those who encounter them.

Community events centered around snowmen joining the battle have become festive traditions in various regions. Snowman festivals and competitions encourage participants to unleash their creativity and humor as they craft larger-than-life snowmen with eye-catching personalities. These events draw locals and visitors alike, fostering community and shared joy as people marvel at the imaginative and often hilarious snowman creations. From the traditional to the avant-garde, the snowmen on display become a testament to the boundless creativity that winter's frozen canvas inspires.

The whimsical idea of snowmen participating in combat is not without its difficulties. The construction of elaborate snowmen requires skill and patience, and the availability of suitable snow is only sometimes guaranteed. Creative alternatives, such as inflatable or artificial snowmen, play in regions with sparse snowfall. While these substitutes lack the ephemeral charm of natural snow, they offer an opportunity for individuals in snow-deprived areas to partake in the festive fun and contribute their humorous interpretations to the snowman tradition.

The evolution of technology has also been aided by advancements in snowmen participating in combat. For instance, the fabrication of lit snowmen that come to life in the nighttime scenery is made possible by outdoor lighting. Solar-powered or LED lights embedded within the snowman's design add a magical glow to these frosty figures, turning them into luminous allies or adversaries that captivate audiences with their festive brilliance. Technology integration expands the possibilities for creativity, allowing dynamic and interactive snowman displays that enchant passersby.

In conclusion, when snowmen join the battle, winter transforms into a whimsical playground where imagination, creativity, and humor reign supreme. The tradition adds a touch of magic to the timeless practice of crafting snowmen, turning these frozen figures into lively participants in the winter narrative. Whether engaged in backyard skirmishes, community competitions, or illuminated nighttime displays, the concept of snowmen joining the battle celebrates the joy of winter play and the enchanting allure of frosty companions taking center stage in the wintry festivities.

CHAPTER 9

Winter Wonderland Chuckles

Polar Bear Comedy Hour

In the vast, icy landscapes of the Arctic, where the bitter cold meets the pristine beauty of snow-covered terrain, a peculiar and endearing tradition unfolds—the Polar Bear Comedy Hour. Far removed from the stoic image often associated with these majestic creatures, the concept of a comedic interlude in the world of polar bears adds a whimsical touch to the icy realms they call home. The idea of a Polar Bear Comedy Hour may seem fanciful. Still, it encapsulates the human fascination with nature's wonders and the imaginative ways we weave humor into the fabric of our interactions with the animal kingdom.

The most giant land carnivores on Earth, polar bears, are typically perceived as symbols of Arctic strength and resilience. However, the notion of a Polar Bear Comedy Hour challenges this conventional view, offering a lighthearted lens to appreciate these magnificent creatures. The comedy hour is not a literal gathering of polar bears engaging in stand-up routines but a symbolic exploration of their behavior and interactions' playful and often humorous aspects.

Central to the Polar Bear Comedy Hour is the observation of polar bear antics that evoke laughter and a sense of camaraderie when viewed through a human lens. For instance, the playful frolicking of polar bear cubs as they tumble and roll in the snow mirrors the exuberance of children engaged in a game of tag. The awkward yet endearing waddle of a full-grown polar bear navigating icy terrain adds a touch of humor to their majestic presence, humanizing them in our eyes.

The comedy unfolds against the stark backdrop of the Arctic, where the pristine whiteness of the snow provides a stage for polar bear playfulness. Rolling in the snow, engaging in mock battles, or sliding down icy slopes, these antics become a form of entertainment that captures the imagination. Through the lens of humor, we connect with these Arctic inhabitants on a more relatable level, appreciating the lighter side of their existence in an environment that demands strength and resilience.

The juxtaposition of the formidable nature of polar bears with their playful behavior is a reminder that even the most powerful creatures in the animal kingdom have moments of lightness and joy. The Polar Bear Comedy Hour invites us to look beyond the fearsome reputation and witness the multifaceted nature of these Arctic giants. It is a testament to the ability of the heart to surprise and delight, offering a glimpse into the intricate balance of strength and vulnerability that defines the lives of polar bears.

While the concept of a Polar Bear Comedy Hour may be a human invention, it reflects our deep-seated desire to connect emotionally with the animal kingdom. We bridge the gap between species through humor, recognizing universal elements of play, curiosity, and joy. In attributing a sense of comedy to the lives of polar bears, we acknowledge our shared capacity for pleasure and the importance of finding fun moments even in the harshest environments.

The Polar Bear Comedy Hour is not limited to physical interactions in the Arctic; it extends to wildlife documentaries and conservation efforts. Filmmakers and researchers often capture the lighter side of polar bear behavior, presenting it to audiences worldwide. These graphic tales provide an insight into the amusing world of polar bears, encouraging empathy and a sense of connection that knows no geographical bounds. Through the lens of humor, these documentaries become a powerful tool for conservation, reminding us of the importance of preserving the habitats that allow these creatures to exhibit their natural behaviors.

In the digital age, the Polar Bear Comedy Hour finds new expression through social media and online platforms. Captivating videos and images of polar bear antics circulate widely, becoming viral sensations that captivate audiences globally. Social media users post these hilarious Arctic situations, bringing joy and fun while drawing attention to the difficulties polar bears endure due to climate change. The Polar Bear Comedy Hour turns the internet into a virtual stage, uniting people worldwide in a shared love of nature's lighter side.

The idea of humor in the animal kingdom is not exclusive to polar bears; it extends to various species that exhibit playful and amusing behaviors. From the acrobatic leaps of dolphins to the comical dances of birds during courtship, nature is replete with animals engaging in activities that evoke laughter and wonder. The human inclination to find humor in the natural world reflects our deep-seated affinity for the creatures with whom we share the planet.

Beyond its amusement, the Polar Bear Comedy Hour also serves a crucial conservation purpose. Polar bears face significant threats due to climate change, melting ice, and diminishing food sources. By showcasing the playful and endearing aspects of opposite bear behavior, conservationists hope to inspire a sense of urgency and empathy among the public. The emotional connection forged through humor catalyzes action, encouraging individuals to contribute to conservation efforts and support initiatives to preserve the Arctic ecosystem.

In conclusion, the Polar Bear Comedy Hour is a symbolic exploration of the lighter side of nature, inviting us to find humor in the lives of one of the planet's most iconic and influential creatures. This imaginative concept transcends the physical boundaries of the Arctic, permeating wildlife documentaries, social media, and conservation efforts. By recognizing the playful and endearing aspects of polar bear behavior, we not only share moments of laughter but also cultivate a deeper connection with the natural world. The Polar Bear Comedy Hour becomes a celebration of the resilience, adaptability, and joy that persist even in the face of environmental challenges, encouraging us to value and preserve the marvels of the Arctic and the creatures that call it home.

Penguin Puns and Icy Improv

In the frosty realms of the Southern Hemisphere, where icy landscapes meet the boundless expanse of the ocean, a delightful tradition unfolds—the world of Penguin Puns and Icy Improv. With their endearing waddle and comical antics, Penguins become unwitting stars in a whimsical performance that marries the charm of wordplay with the improvisational spirit of the frozen landscape they call home. This tradition, though seemingly lighthearted, unveils the playful personalities of these resilient birds and underscores the human fascination with infusing humor into the wonders of the natural world.

Penguin Puns and Icy Improv brings forth the notion that penguins, with their distinctive appearance and amusing behaviors, lend themselves to a comedic narrative. Wordplay and puns centered around penguin-themed humor become a playful way to engage with these flightless birds, highlighting their quirky charm. From quips about their tuxedo-like plumage to jests about their synchronized waddling, penguin puns create a unique form of linguistic amusement that resonates with audiences of all ages.

The humor extends beyond mere wordplay to embrace the physical comedy inherent in penguin behavior. The iconic waddle of penguins, a consequence of their short legs and upright posture, becomes a source of endless amusement. Observing a group of penguins navigate the icy terrain with a synchronized rhythm resembles a comedic ballet, prompting onlookers to envision a penguin-led dance troupe rehearsing a chilly routine. The Icy Improv comes to life as penguins engage in playful antics, sliding across the ice on their bellies or engaging in mock courtship displays that add a touch of amusement to their daily lives.

Penguin Puns and Icy Improv also find expression in popular culture, permeating literature, cartoons, and social media. Animated penguins, brought to life with witty dialogue and humorous situations, become beloved characters that capture the imaginations of audiences worldwide. Social media platforms abound with penguin memes and videos, showcasing their endearing personalities and providing a steady stream of comedic relief. The digital realm becomes a virtual stage for the ongoing performance of Penguin Puns and Icy Improv, connecting people globally through shared laughter.

The tradition is not confined to linguistic play and digital humor; it extends to real-world encounters with penguins in their natural habitats. Wildlife enthusiasts and researchers often find themselves enchanted by the entertaining behaviors of penguins, whether it's the curious approach of a penguin chick or the amusing interactions between adult birds. The Icy Improv of penguins observed firsthand becomes a testament to the resilience and adaptability of these charismatic creatures in the face of challenging environments.

Community events centered around Penguin Puns and Icy Improv bring people together to celebrate the playful side of penguins. Penguin-themed festivals and competitions encourage participants to showcase their creative flair through puns, jokes, and theatrical performances inspired by these charming birds. These events foster a sense of camaraderie as individuals unite in their appreciation for the comedic potential of penguins and the joy they bring to our collective consciousness.

The appeal of Penguin Puns and Icy Improv lies in their ability to humanize these avian inhabitants of the Southern Hemisphere. By attributing characteristics of humor, playfulness, and even theatricality to penguins, we create a bridge between their world and ours, fostering a sense of connection and empathy. The tradition becomes a lens through which we explore nature's lighter side, appreciating the animal kingdom's innate charm and finding common ground through shared laughter.

Like any humor, the secret to Penguin Puns and Icy Improv's success is its capacity to cut over linguistic and cultural barriers. Puns naturally depend on linguistic subtleties, but comedy always finds a home since penguins are such universally likable creatures. The visual comedy of penguin behaviors, captured in images and videos, transcends language, becoming a universal language of joy that sparks laughter across diverse audiences.

The lighthearted tradition of Penguin Puns and Icy Improv takes on added significance as it fosters awareness and appreciation for penguin conservation. Penguins, facing threats such as climate change, overfishing, and habitat destruction, benefit from the attention drawn to their playful personas. The humor surrounding penguins becomes a powerful tool for raising awareness about these birds' challenges and motivating action to safeguard their environments and guarantee their survival in the face of environmental changes.

In conclusion, Penguin Puns and Icy Improv offer a delightful and imaginative lens through which to view the endearing world of penguins. The tradition, blending linguistic play with the physical comedy of penguin behavior, captures the human fascination with infusing humor into the wonders of the natural world. Whether through wordplay, real-world encounters, or community celebrations, the tradition fosters a sense of connection, empathy, and shared joy, highlighting the importance of laughter in our relationship with the charming and resilient inhabitants of the icy Southern Hemisphere.

Frozen Lake Antics

In the heart of winter, when lakes succumb to the frigid embrace of icy temperatures, a magical transformation occurs—the stage is set for the enchanting theater of Frozen Lake Antics. What was once a serene expanse of still water becomes a playground for winter mischief and delight. From impromptu ice-skating escapades to the curious footprints of adventurous wildlife, the frozen lake is a canvas for many antics that capture the season's essence.

Ice skating is one of the most iconic and universally cherished activities on a frozen lake. As temperatures plummet and a crystalline layer of ice blankets the water's surface, individuals of all ages don blades and glide across the icy expanse. The sound of skates carving delicate patterns into the ice becomes a symphony of winter joy, echoing across the snowy landscape. Frozen Lake Antics, in this context, embody the sheer exhilaration and freedom that come with the rhythmic dance of ice skates on a winter's day.

The frozen lake, however, is not solely the domain of human revelry; it hosts diverse characters engaging in their brand of winter antics. Emboldened by the icy platform, wildlife leaves behind a tapestry of tracks and trails that tell tales of their nocturnal wanderings. Squirrel footprints, delicate bird imprints, and the distinctive markings of a rabbit's hop add an element of mystery and intrigue to the frozen canvas. The lake, frozen in time, is a testament to its wild inhabitants' secret lives.

Frozen Lake Antics also extends to the realm of artistic expression. As temperatures dip and frost forms intricate patterns on the icy surface, creative individuals seize the opportunity to transform the lake into a winter art gallery. Detailed ice sculptures emerge, fashioned by skilled hands that carve ethereal forms from the frozen medium. These ephemeral masterpieces, illuminated by the soft glow of winter moonlight or strategically placed lights, elevate the frozen lake into a realm where nature and art converge in a dazzling display.

As communities celebrate the season, the frozen lake becomes a stage for lighthearted games and competitions. From impromptu hockey matches to elaborate ice-fishing derbies, the snowy expanse becomes a communal gathering place where laughter and camaraderie abound. Families build snowmen along the lake's edge, infusing the icy landscape with whimsy as these frosty figures stand sentinel over the frozen domain. In this communal celebration, the frozen lake becomes more than a natural feature—it transforms into a hub of winter activity and shared merriment.

The thrill of Frozen Lake Antics also extends into the realm of unconventional winter sports. Adventurous individuals, armed with kites and snowboards, harness the power of winter winds to glide across the frozen surface. The juxtaposition of the serene, snow-covered landscape and the speed of these winter athletes creates a dynamic spectacle that is as exhilarating as it is visually captivating. Frozen Lake Antics, in this context, become a fusion of nature's beauty and human ingenuity.

As day turns to night, the frozen lake takes on a new dimension of enchantment. Ice lanterns and luminaries dot the landscape, casting a soft and ethereal glow on the icy surface. The stillness of the winter night is interrupted only by the muffled sounds of laughter and the scrape of blades on ice as individuals continue to revel in the enchanting atmosphere. The frozen lake, bathed in the soft luminescence of winter lights, becomes a captivating scene from a storybook—a place where the season's magic comes to life.

But Frozen Lake Antics has its perils and difficulties. Safety becomes the most important consideration when the temperature and the state of the ice change. Local communities and authorities frequently play a critical role in ensuring that people can enjoy the frozen lake appropriately. Signs, warnings, and safety measures aim to balance the joy of winter activities and the need for caution in the face of unpredictable ice conditions. While captivating, the allure of the frozen lake requires a respectful and informed approach to ensure the safety of those who partake in its seasonal festivities.

In the age of technology, Frozen Lake Antics finds new expressions through social media and online platforms. Captivating images and videos of winter escapades on frozen lakes circulate widely, connecting people across the globe in a shared celebration of winter wonder. Social media users share moments of joy, creativity, and adventure, turning the frozen lake into a virtual stage where the season's magic is shared with a global audience. The virtual world takes on the charm of the ice lake and invites people to watch and take part in the wintertime fun from the comfort of their screens.

In conclusion, Frozen Lake Antics encapsulates the spirit of winter in a captivating tableau of play, beauty, and community. From the timeless joy of ice skating to the creative expressions of art and sport, the frozen lake is a central stage for the season's festivities. The antics that unfold on this rigid canvas capture the essence of winter, inviting individuals to partake in the magic of the season and forge lasting memories in the chill of the icy landscape. As communities gather and individuals embark on their winter adventures, the frozen lake symbolizes seasonal delight. In this place, nature and human creativity converge to celebrate the wonders of winter.

CHAPTER 10

Wrapping Paper Mishaps

The Great Gift Wrapping Comedy Show

A unique and often comical tradition takes center stage in the middle of the holiday season's chaos—the Great Gift Wrapping Comedy Show. What begins as a practical task of concealing carefully chosen presents soon evolves into a lighthearted performance, where rolls of wrapping paper become the script, and tape dispensers take on supporting roles. This festive tradition not only showcases gift givers' creativity and imagination but also transforms wrapping into a joyous celebration filled with laughter and merriment.

The Great Gift Wrapping Comedy Show commences as individuals set the stage with various wrapping materials, from festive paper adorned with seasonal motifs to ribbons, bows, and tags. The act of wrapping itself becomes a form of creative expression, with each fold and tuck adding a layer of anticipation to the surprise that lies within. As scissors cut through the paper and tape is dispensed with precision, the mundane task of wrapping transitions into a theatrical performance, setting the scene for holiday cheer.

One of the comedic highlights of the Great Gift Wrapping Comedy Show is the perennial struggle with wrapping paper. As individuals grapple with unruly rolls that seem to have a mind of their own, the otherwise straightforward act of wrapping takes on an amusing twist. Laughter erupts as attempts to cut a straight line result in jagged edges, and the seemingly simple task of folding corners becomes a game of precision akin to a theatrical slapstick routine. The crinkling of paper and the gentle tearing of tape become the soundtrack to a comedy of errors, a symphony of holiday mishaps that only adds to the festive atmosphere.

The art of gift wrapping extends beyond the mere concealment of presents; it becomes an opportunity for individuals to showcase their unique style and flair. The choices of wrapping paper, color schemes, and decorative elements reflect the giver's personality, turning each wrapped gift into a mini-masterpiece. Some opt for classic elegance with coordinated ribbons and bows, while others embrace a more whimsical approach, incorporating playful patterns and unconventional materials. The result is a visually stunning array of gifts that set the stage for the grand unveiling during holiday festivities.

The Great Gift, Wrapping Comedy Show, gains an added layer of humor as gift-givers navigate the challenge of wrapping unconventional shapes and sizes. A comedic dance ensues as boxes contort and bulge beneath the wrapping paper. Disguising an irregularly shaped gift becomes a puzzle, with individuals employing creative folding techniques and copious amounts of tape to ensure a neatly wrapped package. The sight of a miracle that defies conventional wrapping norms often elicits smiles and chuckles, turning the act of unwrapping into a delightful surprise in itself.

Part of the charm of the Great Gift Wrapping Comedy Show lies in its universality. Individuals from all walks of life, regardless of age or background, find themselves caught up in the holiday hilarity as they attempt to tame wayward ribbons or wrestle with stubborn tape. The shared experience of navigating the wrapping challenges becomes a bonding moment, fostering a sense of camaraderie among gift givers who can commiserate over the trials and tribulations of the wrapping process.

Community events and competitions centered around gift wrapping elevate the tradition to a new level of festive entertainment. The Great Gift, Wrapping Comedy Show, becomes a public spectacle as participants, armed with rolls of paper and determined to outdo one another, engage in friendly rivalries to create the most elaborately wrapped gifts. Judges and spectators alike revel in the creativity on display, from intricately folded origami-style covering to thematic presentations that tell a story with each carefully placed ribbon. These events showcase the artistry of gift wrapping and bring communities together in shared laughter and holiday spirit.

The Great Gift Wrapping Comedy Show finds new expression through social media platforms in the digital age. Users share images and videos of their wrapping adventures, transforming wrapping into a virtual performance that resonates with a global audience. Hashtags and challenges related to gift wrapping become viral, encouraging individuals to showcase their creativity and share in the collective joy of holiday hilarity. The virtual world continues the festive tradition, connecting people across distances and celebrating the art of gift giving in a lighthearted and humorous way.

Beyond the laughter and camaraderie, the Great Gift Wrapping Comedy Show serves a deeper purpose in enhancing the overall holiday experience. Wrapping gifts becomes a labor of love, a tangible expression of thoughtfulness and care. The time and effort invested in creating beautifully wrapped presents convey a sense of anticipation and excitement, building a sense of wonder for both the giver and the recipient. The laughter shared during the wrapping process becomes a shared memory, adding to the warmth and joy of the holiday season.

In conclusion, the Great Gift Wrapping Comedy Show transforms a seemingly mundane task into a festive tradition filled with laughter, creativity, and shared merriment. As individuals engage in gift wrapping, they unwittingly become performers in a holiday spectacle that transcends age and background. The mishaps and triumphs of the wrapping process add humor to the season and create lasting recollections that add to the intricate fabric of holiday traditions. In the grand theater of the Great Gift Wrapping Comedy Show, the joy of giving takes center stage, and the act of wrapping becomes a cherished part of the holiday celebration.

Tape Tantrums and Ribbon Riot

In the annual holiday symphony of gift wrapping, a delightful and often humorous tradition takes center stage—the Tape Tantrums and Ribbon Riot. What begins as a seemingly straightforward task of adorning gifts with festive embellishments transforms into a comical performance, complete with tangled tape, unruly ribbons, and the occasional festive fiasco. This festive tradition highlights the playful side of the holiday season and invites participants to embrace the inevitable mishaps and laughter that accompany the art of gift wrapping.

The Tape Tantrums and Ribbon Riot commence as gift-givers, armed with rolls of tape and an array of colorful ribbons, set out to conquer the challenge of creating beautifully adorned presents. The first act unfolds with the unspooling of video, which often takes on a life of its own. Tangles, twists, and unexpected stickiness become the hallmarks of tape tantrums, transforming the straightforward act of securing wrapping paper into a whimsical dance with this often-unruly adhesive companion.

The struggle with tape is a technical challenge and a rite of passage in the gift-wrapping journey. As individuals attempt to tear off the desired video length, the tape dispenser seems to have its agenda, offering either too little or too much adhesive in a naughty game of hide-and-seek. Laughter ensues as gift givers find themselves in a sticky situation, wrestling with tape that seems determined to foil their festive endeavors. In these moments, the Tape Tantrums become an unintentional yet endearing part of the holiday ritual.

The Ribbon Riot, the second act in this whimsical tradition, introduces a new cast of characters to the holiday stage. With their glossy sheen and vibrant hues, Ribbons become the prima donnas of the gift-wrapping performance. However, coaxing ribbons into graceful bows and elegant curls can be a task filled with surprises and, occasionally, a touch of rebellion. Gift givers find themselves entangled in a riot of ribbons as they attempt to achieve the perfect bow or embellish their presents with festive flair.

The Ribbon Riot takes on added complexity when multiple ribbons are introduced into the equation. The challenge of coordinating colors, widths, and textures becomes a creative problem, and the result is often a riotous explosion of ribbons that adds joyful chaos to the visual landscape of wrapped gifts. The playful interplay of stripes celebrates diversity, turning each present into a unique expression of creativity and individuality amid the holiday festivities.

Part of the charm of Tape Tantrums and Ribbon Riot lies in the universality of the experience. Gift givers of all ages and backgrounds find themselves caught up in the holiday hilarity as they navigate the intricacies of tape and ribbons. The shared moments of frustration and laughter become a bonding experience, fostering a sense of camaraderie among individuals who can commiserate over the trials and tribulations of the gift-wrapping process. In this context, the joy of the holiday season is not only found in the perfectly wrapped gift but also in the shared laughter and connection forged through the Tape Tantrums and Ribbon Riot.

Community events and competitions centered around gift wrapping elevate the tradition to a communal celebration of creativity and humor. The Tape Tantrums and Ribbon Riot become public spectacles as participants, armed with rolls of tape and a kaleidoscope of ribbons, engage in friendly rivalries to create the most elaborately adorned gifts. Judges and spectators alike revel in the imaginative and often hilarious presentations, from avant-garde ribbon sculptures to intricate tape mosaics. These events transform the act of gift wrapping into a festive performance that brings communities together in shared laughter and holiday spirit.

In the digital age, the Tape Tantrums and Ribbon Riot find new expression through social media platforms. Users share images and videos of their wrapping adventures, transforming wrapping into a virtual performance that resonates with a global audience. Hashtags and challenges related to tape and ribbon antics become viral sensations, encouraging individuals to showcase their creativity and share in the collective joy of holiday hilarity. The internet space is an extension of the holiday custom, bridging geographical gaps and honoring the art of gift-giving in a fun and playful manner.

Beyond the laughter and camaraderie, Tape Tantrums and Ribbon Riot serve a deeper purpose in enhancing the overall holiday experience. The gift wrapping becomes a labor of love, a tangible expression of thoughtfulness and care. The time and effort invested in creating beautifully adorned presents convey a sense of anticipation and excitement, building a sense of wonder for both the giver and the recipient. The shared experience of navigating the wrapping challenges becomes a shared memory, adding to the warmth and joy of the holiday season.

In conclusion, Tape Tantrums and Ribbon Riot are joyful and humorous traditions that transform the act of gift wrapping into a festive celebration. As individuals engage in dressing, they unwittingly become performers in a holiday spectacle that transcends age and background. The mishaps and triumphs of the wrapping process add humor to the season and create lasting recollections that add to the intricate fabric of holiday traditions. In the grand theater of Tape Tantrums and Ribbon Riot, the joy of giving takes center stage, and wrapping becomes a cherished and entertaining part of the holiday celebration.

The Gift of Laughter

In the tapestry of human experiences, few threads weave a tapestry as vibrant and enduring as the gift of laughter. Laughter, which can transcend cultural boundaries, age differences, and individual quirks, is a universal language that unites people in shared moments of joy and delight. The essence of this gift lies not only in its spontaneous eruptions during moments of humor but also in the intentional cultivation of a lighthearted spirit that weaves through the fabric of our daily lives.

Laughter is a powerful force that serves as a bridge, connecting people in ways that words often cannot. It is a gift that transcends language barriers, enabling communication beyond the confines of spoken or written expression. The shared experience of laughter fosters a sense of camaraderie, creating bonds that endure through the ups and downs of life. Through witty banter, clever jokes, or the infectious joy of genuine amusement, laughter becomes a universal connector that unites individuals, fostering a sense of community and shared humanity.

The gift of laughter is not limited to scripted jokes or rehearsed punchlines; it often finds its roots in the spontaneity of everyday life. Simple moments of humor, whether from amusing anecdotes, unexpected situations, or the delightful antics of children and pets, can elevate the human spirit. The ability to find humor in the ordinary transforms mundane routines into opportunities for joy. In these moments, laughter becomes a precious gift, a reminder that humor and good times can still exist despite life's difficulties.

Humor, as the catalyst for laughter, takes on myriad forms, reflecting the diverse and multifaceted nature of the human experience. It may manifest as clever wordplay, physical comedy, or the gentle art of wit. The beauty of humor lies in its subjectivity; what one finds amusing, another may not. Yet, in this diversity of comedic tastes, the gift of laughter remains an inclusive and democratic force, inviting individuals to appreciate the richness of varied perspectives and to find common ground in shared moments of merriment.

The gift of laughter extends beyond personal connections to encompass the broader realms of societal and cultural contexts. Comedy, as a genre of entertainment, serves as a mirror reflecting the values, norms, and idiosyncrasies of a given society. Satire, parody, and humorous commentary become vehicles for social critique, offering a lens through which to view the world with a discerning yet light-hearted gaze. In this way, the gift of laughter becomes a tool for introspection and societal self-awareness, encouraging individuals to engage with the complexities of the human experience in a spirit of playful inquiry.

In interpersonal relationships, the gift of laughter becomes a powerful ally in navigating challenges and fostering resilience. Shared laughter acts as a salve for wounds, diffusing tension and creating a space for understanding. It becomes a coping mechanism during difficult times, a reminder that even in adversity, there is strength in finding moments of joy. The ability to laugh together, whether in times of celebration or sorrow, fortifies the bonds between individuals, offering a shared language of compassion and support.

The therapeutic benefits of laughter are well-documented, with laughter yoga, laughter clubs, and humor therapy gaining recognition for their positive impact on mental and physical well-being. As a form of natural medicine, Laughter releases endorphins, reduces stress hormones, and promotes relaxation. The gift of laughter, in this sense, becomes a holistic approach to health, promoting emotional resilience and contributing to a positive outlook on life.

The intentional cultivation of a humorous perspective is a gift that individuals can bestow upon themselves and others. The choice to view life through a lens of humor is an empowering act that invites resilience in the face of adversity. This gift involves finding amusement in external circumstances and developing the capacity to laugh at oneself—a form of self-compassion that acknowledges the imperfections and quirks that make each person uniquely human. Embracing a sense of humor becomes a transformative gift, enabling individuals to navigate life with a lightness of spirit that transcends challenges and nurtures a resilient mindset.

In the grand tapestry of human existence, the gift of laughter is a timeless and universal treasure. It is a gift that brings people together, transcending differences and fostering a sense of connection. Whether shared in moments of spontaneous joy or cultivated intentionally as a tool for resilience and well-being, laughter becomes a source of light in life's journey. As individuals exchange the gift of laughter, they create a more compassionate, understanding, and joy-filled world—a world where the threads of humor weave a tapestry that celebrates the shared human experience.

CHAPTER 11

Creative Gift Ideas
– with a Twist

Gift-Giving Gone Wild

In the tapestry of human traditions, few practices embody the spirit of generosity and celebration as vividly as the phenomenon of Gift-Giving Gone Wild. In certain circumstances, what begins as a heartfelt gesture of sharing joy and expressing affection can evolve into an extravagant spectacle of excess and surprise. Fueled by a desire to create memorable and elegant moments, this tradition blurs the lines between thoughtful giving and an unabashed pursuit of the extraordinary. While the intentions behind such grand gestures are often rooted in love and goodwill, the escalation of gift-giving to wild proportions raises questions about the true essence of the act and the impact it has on both givers and recipients.

At the heart of Gift-Giving, Gone Wild is the desire to create moments of sheer astonishment and delight. The notion of going beyond conventional gifts and surprising loved ones with extraordinary presents has become a cultural phenomenon, fueled in part by the influence of social media and the desire to showcase these extravagant acts to a global audience. The act of gift-giving, once a private and intimate exchange, has taken on a performative quality, with individuals vying to outdo each other in the realm of creativity, luxury, and sheer astonishment.

While the intention to create moments of joy is commendable, the wild nature of Gift-Giving Gone Wild raises questions about the expectations and pressures it places on both givers and recipients. The emphasis on the wow factor can sometimes overshadow the sentiment behind the gift, creating an environment where the value of a present is measured in its shock value rather than its emotional resonance. Pursuing ever-grander talents may inadvertently contribute to a culture where material excess becomes the focus, overshadowing the true spirit of generosity and connection.

In the age of social media, Gift-Giving Gone Wild takes on a performative dimension. Individuals document and share their extravagant gift-giving moments, turning what was once a personal exchange into a public spectacle. While this can inspire and entertain, it also contributes to the normalization of over-the-top gift-giving as a societal expectation. The pressure to create viral-worthy moments may lead to a cycle of one-upmanship, where giving becomes more about the external validation it receives than the genuine joy it brings to the recipient.

The financial implications of Gift-Giving Gone Wild must be addressed. Pursuing extravagant gifts often comes with a hefty price tag, potentially straining personal finances and leading to a culture of conspicuous consumption. The desire to outshine previous offerings or meet societal expectations may drive individuals to go to extreme lengths, inadvertently contributing to a culture of material excess and financial strain and giving, which should be a joyous and thoughtful expression, risks being overshadowed by the financial burden associated with maintaining a wild standard of gift-giving.

Moreover, the impact of Gift-Giving Gone Wild extends beyond the immediate exchange. The expectations set by extravagant gifts may inadvertently create a sense of obligation or comparison among recipients. Individuals who receive such grand gestures may feel pressured to reciprocate in kind, leading to a cycle of escalating expectations that can be emotionally and financially draining. In this way, the wild nature of gift-giving can inadvertently transform a joyous tradition into a source of stress and anxiety.

Despite these worries, it's critical to understand that Gift-Giving Gone Wild has positive aspects. The desire to create memorable and extraordinary moments reflects a genuine intention to bring joy and surprise to loved ones. These extravagant gifts are often driven by deep affection and the wish to express gratitude or grandly celebrate special occasions. The difficulty is striking a balance between the desire for extravagance and the thoughtful consideration of the recipient's needs and preferences.

As individuals navigate the realm of Gift-Giving Gone Wild, there is an opportunity to reclaim the essence of the tradition. Thoughtfulness, personal connection, and understanding the recipient's preferences can guide gift-givers in creating meaningful moments without succumbing to excess pressure. Meaningful gifts need not be extravagant; they can be simple, thoughtful, and reflective of the bond between the giver and the recipient. By emphasizing the sentiment and personal connection behind the gift, individuals can ensure that giving remains a joyful and genuine expression of love and appreciation.

In conclusion, Gift-Giving Gone Wild is a complex and multifaceted tradition that reflects contemporary society's evolving dynamics of generosity and celebration. While the desire to create extraordinary moments is rooted in love and goodwill, the wild nature of extravagant gift-giving raises questions about its impact on individuals and the culture. By re-evaluating the emphasis on shock value and external validation, individuals can reclaim the essence of gift-giving as a meaningful and thoughtful expression of connection and joy. In creating memorable moments, the true gift lies not in the extravagance of the present but in the heartfelt intention and personal relationship that underlies the act of giving.

The Art of Wrapping Oddly-Shaped Presents

In the enchanting world of gift-giving, wrapping presents becomes a delightful expression of creativity and ingenuity. Yet, when faced with the challenge of wrapping oddly shaped gifts, the artistry of gift wrapping takes on a new level of complexity. The conventional square or rectangular box gives way to irregular shapes and dimensions, presenting gift wrappers with unique challenges. The art of wrapping oddly shaped presents is an intricate dance between precision and adaptability, where folds, tucks, and tape transform into tools of artistic expression.

The journey of wrapping oddly shaped presents begins with a contemplative gaze upon the unconventional form. Whether it's the curves of a vase, the angles of a sculpture, or the asymmetry of an artisanal item, the wrapper must first decipher the inherent geometry of the gift. Unlike the straightforward task of wrapping a box, the irregularity of the object demands a thoughtful approach—one that requires an understanding of the unique contours and dimensions that make the present distinct.

The selection of wrapping materials becomes a crucial step in covering odd shapes. Flexible materials like tissue paper become allies to smooth out uneven surfaces and accentuate the gift's form. With its kaleidoscope of colors and patterns, wrapping paper becomes a canvas for creativity, transforming the odd shape into a work of art. The choice of ribbon, bows, and decorative elements adds a finishing touch, turning the wrapped present into a visual delight that captivates even before the reveal.

The cornerstone of wrapping oddly shaped presents lies in adaptability. Unlike the clean lines of a square box, these gifts often defy the conventions of symmetry, demanding a flexible and intuitive approach. The wrapper must navigate the contours with a delicate touch, adjusting folds and creases to accommodate the unique shape. In this dance of adaptation, the tape becomes a versatile ally, holding together the seams and ensuring that the wrapping adheres to the gift's idiosyncrasies.

The art of wrapping odd shapes extends beyond the visual appeal to encompass the tactile experience of unwrapping. The recipient, faced with a gift that deviates from the norm, embarks on a sensory journey as they explore the textures and forms beneath the wrapping. The anticipation builds with each unfolding layer, creating a sense of excitement and curiosity that adds to the magic of the unwrapping experience. In this way, the art of wrapping oddly shaped presents becomes a collaborative act between the giver and the recipient, where the wrapping itself becomes an integral part of the gift.

The challenges posed by odd shapes are not without their humorous moments. Wrappers often engage in a playful game of hide-and-seek with tape, attempting to secure unruly corners and edges. The wrapping transforms into a dynamic process, with unexpected folds and tucks, turning the odd shape into a whimsical surprise. Laughter becomes a companion in this creative endeavor as wrappers navigate the playful challenges presented by gifts that defy the conventional norms of wrapping.

Community events and competitions centered around the art of wrapping oddly shaped presents elevate the tradition to a communal celebration of creativity and ingenuity. Wrappers gather to showcase their skills, transforming unconventional objects into beautifully wrapped works of art. Judges and spectators alike marvel at the inventive approaches, from elaborate folding techniques to imaginative use of materials. These events not only celebrate the artistry of wrapping but also foster unity among those passionate about the creative expression of gift-giving.

In the digital age, wrapping oddly shaped presents finds new expressions through social media and online platforms. Wrappers share images and videos of their adventures, turning wrapping into a virtual performance that resonates with a global audience. Hashtags and challenges related to creative wrapping become viral sensations, encouraging individuals to showcase their adaptability and share in the collective joy of mastering the art of wrapping odd shapes. The digital realm extends the festive tradition, connecting people across distances in a shared celebration of creativity.

The art of wrapping oddly shaped presents is not confined to specific occasions but extends throughout the year. Birthdays, anniversaries, and celebrations of all kinds become opportunities to explore the boundaries of creativity in gift presentation. The act of wrapping transforms mundane moments into extraordinary experiences, where the artistic expression enhances the thoughtfulness behind the gift. This way, wrapping odd shapes becomes a timeless and versatile tradition, adapting to the ever-changing landscape of occasions and celebrations.

In conclusion, the art of wrapping oddly shaped presents celebrates creativity, adaptability, and the joyous spirit of gift-giving. Wrappers, armed with an understanding of geometry and a touch of whimsy, embark on a journey to transform irregular forms into beautifully adorned gifts. The challenges posed by odd shapes are met with laughter, ingenuity, and a commitment to creating moments of delight. As odd-shaped presents find their way into the hands of recipients, the art of wrapping becomes a testament to the power of creativity to elevate the simple act of giving into a truly extraordinary experience.

A Comedy of Second Chances

In the grand theater of life, where the curtains rise and fall on the stage of human experiences, the narrative often unfolds as a complex interplay of drama, tragedy, and, occasionally, a delightful Comedy of Second Chances. This particular genre of life's storytelling invites us to witness the whimsical and unexpected twists of fate that grant individuals another shot at redemption, transformation, and the pursuit of happiness. It is a narrative thread woven with the lines of resilience, uncertainty, and the belief that life's follies can offer the most unexpected yet humorous opportunities for rebirth.

The Comedy of Second Chances unfurls as characters find themselves at the crossroads of their narratives, facing challenges, setbacks, or even the consequences of their choices. Within these moments, often perceived as the climax of life's challenges, the curtain lifts on the unexpected encore—the second chance. Whether it be a missed opportunity, a failed endeavor, or a relationship that seemed destined for closure, life, in its infinite wisdom, occasionally beckons the characters to take a bow for an unexpected reprise.

One of the defining features of the Comedy of Second Chances is its element of surprise. Much like a clever plot twist, the unexpected second chance emerges from the wings of life, catching characters off guard and inviting them to reconsider the narrative trajectory. This surprise element injects humor into the storyline, dispelling stereotypes and providing a novel viewpoint on life's challenges. The laughter accompanying these twists is not mockery but a celebration of life's capacity for renewal and the delightful absurdity of the human experience.

The concept of second chances extends beyond individual stories to encompass a broader societal and cultural perspective. In a world that often grapples with issues of forgiveness, redemption, and the possibility of transformation, the Comedy of Second Chances becomes a collective narrative that reflects the potential for growth and renewal on a grand scale. Societal structures, systems, and individuals are entangled in a complex dance of challenges and opportunities, with the promise of a comedic encore waiting in the wings.

At the heart of the Comedy of Second Chances is the theme of resilience. This quality enables people to overcome obstacles, grow from mistakes, and find humor in the face of adversity. It is the ability to laugh at one's foibles, to see the absurdity in life's challenges, and to embrace the unexpected with a light-hearted spirit. This resilience transforms life's inevitable missteps into stepping stones, paving the way for new beginnings and, perhaps, a few comedic anecdotes for the script of life.

The concept of second chances often finds its most poignant expression in relationships. Whether it's rekindling old friendships, the revival of a romance, or the healing of familial bonds, the Comedy of Second Chances is a heartwarming and humorous exploration of human connections. Characters who once stood on opposite sides of a conflict or drifted apart in the currents of life discover that the universe has a sense of humor, bringing them together for an unexpected encore filled with laughter, understanding, and a renewed appreciation for shared histories.

In the workplace, the Comedy of Second Chances reveals itself as professionals navigate the ever-changing landscape of careers. Failed projects, missed promotions, or even career pivots that initially appeared as setbacks become the raw material for a comedic sequel. With its intricate web of relationships and ambitions, the workplace becomes a stage where individuals can embrace the unexpected twists of professional life, finding humor in the face of uncertainty and turning setbacks into stepping stones for career advancement.

The Comedy of Second Chances also shapes community and societal narratives. Societal structures that once seemed resistant to change find themselves amid unexpected transformations. Movements for justice, equality, and social change often embody the essence of this comedic encore, challenging the status quo and offering society a chance to rewrite its narrative with a more inclusive and equitable script. The laughter accompanying these societal shifts is not just a light-hearted chuckle but a collective celebration of the resilience and transformative potential of the human spirit.

In the digital age, the Comedy of Second Chances finds new expressions through social media and online platforms. Individuals share their stories of redemption, growth, and unexpected opportunities, turning the digital realm into a virtual stage for the collective Comedy of Second Chances. Hashtags and online movements centered around resilience and renewal become viral sensations, connecting people across the globe in a shared celebration of life's unexpected encores. The digital space becomes a canvas for the collaborative creation of a global narrative that celebrates the potential for growth, laughter, and renewal.

In conclusion, the Comedy of Second Chances is a whimsical and profound narrative thread that runs through the tapestry of human experiences. It celebrates resilience, renewal, and the unexpected twists that life offers when least expected. Whether played out in individual stories, relationships, workplaces, or societal shifts, the Comedy of The book Second Chances encourages us to take joy in the unanticipated encores that await each of us and to laugh at the ridiculousness of life's obstacles. In this grand theater of existence, where the curtains rise and fall, the Comedy of Second Chances stands as a testament to the enduring resilience of the human spirit and the capacity for laughter even in the face of life's most dramatic plot twists.

Conclusion

In the festive world of "Hilarious Holiday Humor for Kids: Santa's Giggle Factory- A Collection of Holiday Humor," the delightful journey through laughter and merriment concludes as an enchanting gift to both children and the young at heart. This e-book, akin to Santa's sack of presents, overflows with the joyous spirit of the holiday season, offering a collection of whimsical tales, cheerful anecdotes, and playful humor that resonates with the magic of Christmas.

As the last pages unfold, readers find themselves immersed in a world where the magic of the holidays isn't just about presents under the tree but also the gift of laughter shared with loved ones. The e-book succeeds in crafting a heartwarming atmosphere where the joy of Santa and his merry companions permeates every story, creating a tapestry of amusement that captivates readers of all ages.

The diverse range of holiday humor within these digital pages ensures something for everyone, from the mischievous adventures of Santa's elves to the comical escapades of festive characters. The collection seamlessly weaves timeless holiday traditions with a modern sense of humor, making it a delightful read for families gathered around the fireplace or for youngsters eager to experience the season's magic.

Moreover, the e-book's success lies not only in its ability to elicit laughter but also in its capacity to create lasting memories. The stories and jokes, carefully curated for their appeal to young readers, become a shared experience that families can revisit year after year. With its twinkling lights and festive decorations, the holiday season gains an extra layer of joy as the echoes of laughter from the e-book become a cherished part of the seasonal soundtrack.

Essentially, "Hilarious Holiday Humor for Kids: Santa's Giggle Factor- A Collection of Holiday Humor" serves as a virtual ticket to Santa's workshop, where laughter is the most precious gift. The e-book captures the essence of the holiday season, reminding readers that amidst the hustle and bustle, the true magic lies in the shared moments of joy and merriment. As the final pages turn, it leaves behind a warm afterglow, a reminder that the spirit of Santa's laughter lives on, creating a timeless connection between the joyous tales within and the festive hearts of those who explore its delightful contents.

Thank you for buying and reading/listening to our book. If you found this book useful/helpful please take a few minutes and leave a review on the platform where you purchased our book. Your feedback matters greatly to us.